This Book
Presented to

By

Comments

HAPPY MARRIAGES AND STRONG FAMILIES

A Spiritual Journey

Kelley Brigman, PhD

Purple's Edge Media, LLC

Unattributed quotations are by Kelley Brigman.

Publisher's Catalog-in-Publication
(by Quality Books, Inc.)

Brigman, Kelley.
    Happy marriages and strong families : a spiritual journey / by Kelley Brigman. -- 1st ed.
    p. cm.
    Includes bibliographical references.
    LCCN 2011918842
    ISBN-13: 978-0-9815965-6-3
    ISBN-10: 0-9815965-6-8

    1. Families--Religious life. 2. Marriage--Religious aspects--Christianity. 3. Christian life.   I. Title.

    BV4526.3.B75 2012   248.4
                      QBI11-200024

Cover by Mallory Rapp.

Printed in the United States of America

For quantity orders, please contact Purple's Edge Media, LLC

Purple's
Edge Media, LLC

209 Viking Drive
Mankato, Minnesota 56001
Order from www.purplesedgemedia.com

This book is lovingly dedicated to all the people who want to create happy marriages and strong families. It is specifically dedicated to all the:

- Husbands and wives who love, cherish, and honor one another;
- Mothers and fathers who make sacrifices to love and rear their children, and
- Children who honor their families and respect their parents.

TABLE OF CONTENTS

ABOUT THE AUTHOR

Dr. Kelley Brigman has been interested in learning how to create successful families as long as he can remember. His passion for families became his profession. He has spent almost 30 years teaching family relations at Minnesota State University, Mankato where he considered teaching students how to create successful relationships his most important role. Dr. Brigman has also done research in the area of family strengths and family strengths and religion. His interest in religion and family strengths has spanned more than thirty years.

Dr. Brigman is a seminary graduate and spent eleven years in professional ministry. He is a Licensed Marriage and Family Therapist. Dr. Brigman is the author of *Marriage: A Simple Guide to Success,* and several journal articles and magazine articles.

Dr. Brigman is available to conduct workshops on building strong relationships and religion and family strengths, and is also available for interviews, speaking engagements, preaching, readings, and book signings. For more information, see www.kellcybrigman.com and www.purplesedgemedia.com.

ACKNOWLEDGEMENTS

I want to express my appreciation to the many people who have helped me along the journey of writing this book. Above all others, I want to thank my wife. Katie has helped me learn many of the lessons about marriages and families that I have written about in this book. I also appreciate her support and patience during the three years that I have worked on this book, and for helping with editing and some of the technical aspects of the book.

I am deeply indebted to hundreds of psychologists and family scholars and researchers who have provided research and theories that underlie most of the teachings in this book. While the people who have helped are many, Nick Stinnett and John DeFrain stand out because they have been mentors to me in the family strengths approach to family science.

I am thankful to all the friends and colleagues who were willing to read parts of the manuscript and make suggestions and especially to those who have given endorsements.

I am truly grateful for all the people and families from whom I have learned so much through my professional experiences.

Thank you and blessings to all the people who will read this book. If reading this book helps strengthen your marriages and families, I will be rewarded for my work.

Kelley Brigman

DISCLAIMER

This book is designed to educate. It should not be used as the definitive source of information about marriage or other relationships. It is not intended to be a substitute for individual, marital, or family therapy, or for medical, legal, financial, or other professional advice or services. If such services are needed, please consult an appropriate professional. If your relationship is dangerous or abusive, you need to seek professional help immediately.

The recommendations in this book are made without any guarantee. Neither the author nor Purple's Edge Media, LLC shall have liability or responsibility to any person or entity with respect to any loss or damage caused, or allegedly to have been caused, directly or indirectly, by the information contained in this book.

CHAPTER 1

WHERE TO BEGIN:

INTRODUCTION

People have repeatedly told researchers that having a successful family is one of their most important goals in life. Members of the strongest families have also told researchers that their religion is one of their most important sources of family strengths.

This book will teach you how your religion can help you create a successful marriage and strong family. It will specifically teach you which core aspects of the Christian religion are most helpful to families and how you can apply them in your family.

Whether you want to develop your family's fullest potential, begin a marriage on the right foot, or revitalize a troubled relationship, the most basic elements of the Christian religion can help.

About the Book

This book contains information about families that I have learned from my academic training, from my teaching and research, from my experience counseling individuals and families, and from my own life experience. The discussions about religion and family are based on my own research.

In one study, I asked family-life professionals from all over the United States if they thought religion could help people create strong families. A large majority of the respondents said "Yes." They also identified seven core elements of our religion that they believed could be most helpful to families.

In another study, I asked members of families from around the United States to answer questions that were designed to measure religious attitudes and questions that were designed to measure family strengths. Comparing the responses allowed me to observe how peoples' religious attitudes influenced their families.

Religion

This book defines religion as a set of beliefs and practices that help us relate to God. Being religious implies the practice of spiritual discipline through which we challenge ourselves to live according to a standard of truth that is greater than human wisdom such as the Bible and the teachings of the church. Living the Christian life involves applying the principles of our religion in every aspect of our lives and usually involves being part of a culture of faith such as the church.

Who Am I?

You may be wondering who I am that you should read what I have written about families and religion. Christians are careful about selecting the sources of information they let influence their lives, and rightly so.

I am a family scientist trained in the family strengths orientation. I am also a former minister with a seminary degree. I am a practicing Christian.

I have worshipped in all kinds of churches, from St. Peter's in Rome and Westminster Abbey in London, to new thought churches and mainline Protestant churches all over America, as well as small fundamentalist and charismatic churches in the rural South where I grew up. I have found the Spirit of God in all these churches and in the people who worship in them. I accept and honor all Christian traditions. I believe God is with all of us on our spiritual journeys.

My goal in this book is to teach readers how to create happy marriages and strong families by applying the core elements of the Christian religion in their families.

Since I am speaking as a social scientist rather than as a minister or priest, I have been careful not deal with doctrinal, sectarian, or controversial issues. I hope readers will interpret their own beliefs, work with their own religious leaders, and benefit from the support of their own churches. This book will deal with scriptures but only as they relate to marriages and families.

Families have always been important to me. Life did not automatically give me a family or teach me the skills I needed to create one. Even as a small child I watched families and wished I could be married and have a family. Learning how to create a successful marriage and family has been one of the important themes in my life, and one of my greatest challenges.

As an adult, I looked to the teachings of psychology and family science to help me learn how to create a successful family. I even became a family-life professional.

I began my career thinking that a good marriage and strong family were based on the principles of family science and psychology. I believed that when I got my PhD and became a professor of family relations and a marriage and family therapist, I would be able to create a strong family and help other families solve their problems too.

Over time, I began to realize that many of the concepts I had learned in my training did not work very well in my own family, and they did not seem to be helping people I worked with much either.

I also noticed that despite the fact that we have at least one family living course in every high school and college in the land and a counselor on every corner, we have never been so confused about how to create successful marriages and families, or how to be effective parents.

I have learned that many of the principles of family science and psychology are useful for understanding the dynamics of relationships. But the basic principles recommended for creating successful relationships, such as balancing costs and rewards, fairness, justice, negotiation, and compromise, are better suited for running a business or helping diverse people live together in society than for creating happy marriages and strong families.

A successful marriage is more about giving than receiving, more about compassion than negotiation, and more about forgiveness than justice. I have also found that basic religious concepts such as compassion, acceptance, and forgiveness are the most important resources for creating successful families, and are absolutely essential for solving marital and family problems.

I began improving my own marriage by replacing practices such as communication, negotiation, and conflict management with faith and hope, love and grace, respect and honor which are based on the concept of parenthood of God, and forgiveness and reconciliation. Gradually, my wife and I changed from two unhappy people on the brink of divorce to two happy people with a strong marriage.

This book is based on sound psychology and family science, but I have added important Christian concepts that family-life professionals do not usually employ. When the teachings of family science and psychology differ with core Christian elements, I have chosen to follow Christian teachings. For instance, I have replaced concepts such as balancing costs and rewards with the concept of giving all we have to give. Marriage is based on the biblical principle of sowing and reaping: we receive as we have given. I have also replaced the idea that forgiveness can be psychologically unhealthy with Christian teachings about forgiving.

I consider what I have written to be a Christian psychology of marriage and family relationships. I also consider it a micro-psychology of marriage and family because it analyzes the tiny attitudes and behaviors that wash through our relationships and create our successes or failures.

Some people will think that what I have written is idealistic and I agree. Our faith is the source of our highest ideals. These ideals become our reality when we apply them in our lives.

The suggestions in this book actually do work. We can forgive people who have hurt us instead of being resentful and getting even. We can accept people just the way God made them. We can love compassionately. And, when we do, we will grow and our marriages and our families will be stronger.

I will admit that it is not easy to act lovingly or to forgive no matter what others do. I have been learning how to apply what I know about marriages and families in my own marriage for years. I try to practice the concepts I have written about in this book every day. On a good day I give myself about a B-, and on an average day I give myself a C+. I have learned to avoid all D and F behaviors regardless of what my wife does. I sometimes fall short of my goal, but like every other aspect of my Christian life, I try to keep the vision in my mind and keep trying.

I have found that when we are trying to create happy marriages and strong families by applying faith and hope, love and grace, honor and respect, and forgiveness and recon- ciliation, even making a sound C+ can be pretty helpful.

I believe I have been "called" to write this book and that I have been led by the spirit and my faith as I have written. I will admit that the little professor in me often tried to hijack the process and I have had to mark out and rewrite many times. I believe you can let the Spirit lead you as you create a happy marriage and strong family. The teachings of the Bible, the church, and the leadership of the Spirit are our best resources for creating successful marriages and families.

I have grown as I have written this book, and I hope reading it will help you grow. Helping other people create successful marriages and strong families has become my passion and my mission.

You Are the Expert on Your Life

Since you are reading this book you are likely to be interested in your family and in your religion. You are probably someone who has also been influenced—for better or for worse—by advice from professionals.

I want you to know that you are the most important expert on your life, your family, and your religion.

I hope you will consider the ideas in this book, and I hope you will trust yourself to decide how to apply what you learn in your own family. I also encourage you to ask the Spirit to guide you.

How to Read This Book

There is no one way to read this book. Some people may read it all at one setting; others may want to do a chapter at a time so they can digest the ideas and put them into practice.

Since I wrote *Marriage: A Simple Guide to Success,* several women have told me they had read the book to their husbands. Women read self-help books more than men and they talk more than men, but I do hope some husbands have read it to their wives as well. Some couples have told me they have taken turns reading this book to one another.

When couples read a book together they are spending time together and doing things together which are characteristics of a strong family. They are also developing a sense of shared meaning by exposing themselves to the same ideas. The greater the sense of shared meaning couples and families have, the more likely they are to understand themselves and their world the same way, and the more likely they are to have similar values and goals.

While there are benefits to reading this book together, you will miss the point if you read it and begin trying to negotiate changes. I want you to learn that you create your relationships, and it only takes one person to change a relationship—you. Trying to communicate about problems and negotiate changes is one of the problems many people have in their marriages today. It is the nature of the Christian life to do unto others as we would have them do unto us—no matter what others do.

Chapter by Chapter

This book contains nine chapters. This Introduction describes the book, defines religion, and discusses the author's approach. The second chapter describes the relationship between religion and family and briefly discusses how our religion can help us create successful families. The third chapter describes the cycle of creation, the process by which we create everything in our lives, including our families. Chapters four through eight will teach you how to apply the core elements of the Christian religion such as commitment, faith and hope, love and grace, respect and honor, and forgiveness and reconciliation, to create happy marriages and strong families. The conclusion will encourage you to lay aside any weights that hold you back and apply the core elements of your religion to creating successful relationships every day.

Affirmations

Each chapter of this book contains affirmations. Affirmations are positive prayers. They affirm that what we are praying for already exists. For instance, I can say, "God is helping me as I solve this problem and I am thankful." Psalm 23 is a collection of affirmations: "The Lord is my shepherd, I shall not want." Philippians 4:13, "I can do all things through Christ who gives me strength," is an affirmation from the New Testament.

Affirmations have the same spiritual benefits as prayers. They affirm that we believe our prayers are already being answered. "The Spirit is guiding me as I create a successful marriage" is one of my affirmations. It is one way I express my faith as I apply it to my marriage and my family.

Affirmations also help us create what we are affirming. Affirming that "I am a kind, generous, and loving husband," keeps me focused on my goal to be kind, loving, and generous. It affects my life because I become what I think about.

Today we know that we create our lives with our thoughts. We also know that our thoughts develop and train our brains. When we affirm over and over that the Spirit is helping us to be kind and loving husbands and wives, our brains are creating the neural structures we need to be kind and loving spouses.

Prayers and affirmations are especially useful in times of challenge and conflict. When we utilize prayers and affirmations, we open ourselves to the leadership of the Spirit. When we have a disagreement or crisis we can say, "Holy Spirit, be with me now," or "The Spirit is guiding me as I solve this problem." Then we can let the Spirit lead us.

Remember, good affirmations are positive statements. Instead of saying, God, please help me to be a kind and loving husband," I can say, "God is guiding me as I become a kind and loving husband." It is also good to include a statement of thanksgiving. Either, "I am thankful that God is helping me to be a kind and loving husband," or, "God is with me as I create a strong family and I am thankful." You can use the affirmations from this book, and you can write new ones for yourself. I have mine on small cards so I can read and affirm them daily. It helps to have our affirmations written, rehearsed, and ready whenever we need them most.

Affirmations

- God is with me in this moment and in every moment, and I am thankful.

- The Spirit of God is guiding me as I learn how to create successful relationships.

- I always do my best to be a good friend, a good husband (or wife), and a good father or mother.

- There is but one presence and one power in my life and in my relationships—God the omnipotent good.

CHAPTER 2

RELIGION, MARRIAGE, AND FAMILY

> "In you shall all the families of the earth be blessed."
> – Genesis 12:3 NRSV

I remember numerous Sunday mornings when I made the 10-mile trip through Omaha from my home to the church. I was usually concerned about the service, especially the sermon. I was seldom calm, but the city was calm. Different from any other time. On Sunday mornings, the population seemed to be split into two worlds: those who were sleeping late or relaxing at home and those who were making the journey toward their churches. Even the traffic looked different. People were traveling in family groups.

I sometimes wondered which families benefited more: the ones who spent a relaxing day at home together or the ones who went to church. I especially wondered if what went on behind the stained glass windows made families stronger.

At the time, I was a minister and a doctoral student studying family relations at the University of Nebraska - Lincoln. I was also struggling with a failing marriage and with questions about my own faith.

I was interested in family strengths and family strengths research. This was the beginning of my interest in the study of religion and family that has spanned more than thirty years.

Religion and Family

Every society throughout history has had families and some kind of religion. Humans have an innate need to establish intimate connections with God and with other people. Most of us find our deepest meaning and our closest connections within the institutions of religion and family.

Social institutions are organized systems of behavior that help us meet basic human needs. We do not have to figure out how to meet each need individually because institutions help us meet whole clusters of needs.

The Christian religion is a set of beliefs and practices that help us worship and serve God. The Christian religion helps us understand the world, ourselves, and others. It teaches us what is important and what is not, and what is right and what is wrong. Our religion also teaches us how to relate to our husbands and wives, children and parents, friends and neighbors and even our enemies. It teaches us not to kill or hurt people, not to steal, not to tell lies about other people, and not to judge others. It teaches us to love, accept, and forgive.

Most Christians belong to a church which challenges them to live up to a standard greater than themselves and provides a source of social support and models for Christian behaviors. Belonging to a church gives us access to a support system of people who share our values and goals.

The most intimate and meaningful human connections most of us have are usually with other people are usually in our families. It is in our families that we find our deepest sense of satisfaction and our strongest source of emotional stability. Our closest family members are usually our best friends, allies, and partners.

A successful marriage is usually the core of strong families. For most people, marriage offers more benefits—

emotionally and materially—than any other lifestyle. Marriage is the safest of all relationships for both women and men, but especially for women.

Living in families also facilitates our meeting many practical needs ranging from making a living and sharing resources to preparing food, providing clothing, and maintaining a home. Most people do better in every area of their lives because they live in families. The family is by far the best structure for producing and rearing children.

Like owning our own homes, we can depend on our families to meet our needs day after day, year after year.

Does Being Religious Help Families?

Helpful Religious Beliefs and Practices

- Basic religious beliefs such as love, faith, hope, forgiveness, grace, reconciliation, parenthood of God, and divine worth of humans.
- Basic religious life-style of commitment, respon-sibility, giving, and caring for others.
- Shared beliefs, values, and family religious observances.
- Shared church activities.
- Reverence for marriage and family as a sacred lifestyle.
- Support group/network.

- Brigman, *Religion and Family Strengths:
   An Approach to Wellness*, pp. 4-5

Members of strong families around the world have told family researchers that their religion is one of the most important sources of family strengths. We like to believe that Christian couples will automatically create successful marriages and strong families. But it is not quite that simple.

We can think of our religion as potential energy. Christian qualities such as faith and hope, love (compassion), acceptance (grace), respecting and honoring one another, and forgiveness and reconciliation are our most important resources for creating strong families. But we have to understand how these concepts apply to our marriages and families, and we have to apply them with some consistency— even when it is hardest.

Christian teachings are never the only forces affecting our families. We have to compete with other influences in a society that values work and productivity and individual freedom and personal and professional growth over commitment to families.

Being a good husband or wife is a challenge. It is not easy for us to accept everything our spouses do without sometimes thinking our way is better. It is not easy to forgive every time a family member disappoints or offends us. It is sometimes hardest to apply the principles of compassion and forgiveness in our relationships when we need them most.

In spite of the difficulty we have in creating strong families in a challenging environment, the effect of religion can often be the difference between solving a problem and not solving it. Even people who have troubled marriages can usually turn them around when they apply the core elements of their religion to their families.

The simple answer to the question, "Does my religion help strengthen my family?' is "Perhaps." The simple answer to the question, "Can my religion help strengthen my family," is a resounding "Yes."

Who Benefits Most?

My research indicates that one religious attitude—*True Commitment*—is most helpful for building family strengths. Roger Meyer describes True Commitment as "personal faith and devotion, humble evaluation of one's religious life, and a strong conviction in what one believes." People who score high on the True Commitment scale are totally devoted to their religion.

People whose families benefit most from their religion have (1) a deep internal faith, (2) apply their beliefs in their marriages and family relationships, and (3) belong to a church. My research indicates that the combination of these three factors results in the most positive contribution of religion to happy marriages and strong families.

A Deep Internal Faith

People whose families benefit the most from their religion are devoted to their faith. Their motivation to practice their religion in every aspect of their lives comes from their hearts. It is their delight. Most of them pray regularly and ask for leadership from the Spirit. Religion also directs their energies away from being absorbed by self-interest and toward caring for others, especially for family members.

Apply Their Beliefs in Their Families

People who are totally committed to the practice of their faith apply their beliefs in every aspect of their lives. They exhibit Christian attitudes and behaviors that give them a sense of purpose and goals in life and the personal strength they need to achieve them. They do what is right no matter what others do. Even if a family member is angry, people who are totally committed to their families will try to respond lovingly. They follow the big principles of their faith such as the Golden Rule, and they remember that their family members are the neighbor that they are to love as themselves, the brother of whom they are keeper, and the brother whom they are to forgive.

Husbands and wives apply their religion to their families by being committed, kind and loving, and by acting responsibly and caring for one another and for their children, by accepting one another unconditionally, and by forgiving one another when they make mistakes.

Belong to a Church or Religious Organization

People who are committed to their religion are usually involved in a church. They go to services because they want to worship and learn, and because they want to associate with other people who share their beliefs, values, and goals.

Being active in a family-friendly church allows people to be part of a culture that values families. Family-friendly churches have a reverence for families and openly support it. They also support families through beliefs that emphasize commitment, responsibility, giving and caring for others. Family-friendly churches encourage us to apply the principles of our faith to every facet of our lives including our families. Most family-friendly churches also provide programs and services such as family-life education, support groups, and counseling that help strengthen families.

The Tools of the Spirit

Families especially benefit when they apply seven core elements of the Christian religion in their marriages and families: faith, hope, love, grace, parenthood of God, forgiveness, and

Happy Marriages and Strong Families

reconciliation. I call these the tools of the Spirit.

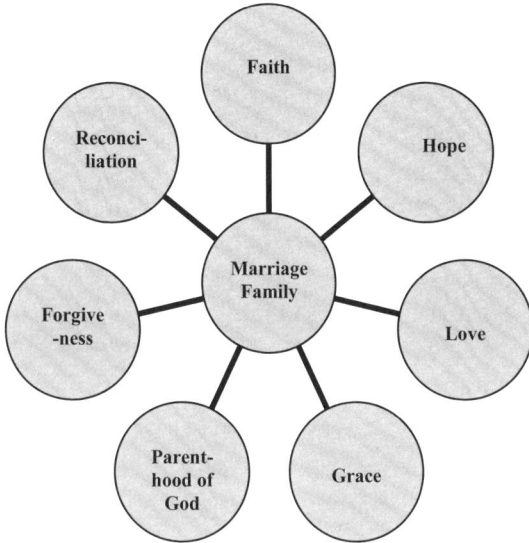

A Simple Guide to Family Strengths

We do not hear much about strong families today, but researchers have found that there are many strong and healthy families. Husbands and wives who are happy being together. Families with children who like one another. Husbands, wives, and children working together. Elderly men and women who have been together for a lifetime taking care of one another.

We could compare strong families to houses. There are many different kinds of houses. Some have more rooms than others; some have larger rooms than others. But all houses need a living space, food preparation space, eating space, sleeping space, and bathroom space.

No matter how different houses are they follow the same principles for stick construction, plumbing, electrical wiring, and ventilation. Building codes are based on principles of construction that work and keep people safe and healthy.

Here is a simple list of characteristics and behaviors of strong families. It is a little long, but understanding what strong families are like can help us understand how to create strong families. I hope readers will use this list as a guide for developing strengths in their own families.

Of course, most members of strong families do not make an A in every category, but members of strong families will make an A or B in most categories. They may make an occasional C, but will probably not make a D or F in any categories, or even engage in any D or F behaviors.

Members of strong families

- Are highly committed to the family and to one another. Husbands and wives can invest totally in their families because they believe they will be together for the rest of their lives. Children know their parents will make a home for them and provide the love, nurture, and support they need.

- Accept one another, love one another compassionately, and forgive one another when they make mistakes. They are kind to one another and honor one another.

- Have a high level of spiritual health. Family members have a strong sense of faith which is often expressed as a strong religious orientation or set of values that gives them a sense of meaning and purpose and direction for their lives.

- Maintain a culture of good will. Strong families are based on a strong sense of cooperation. The family atmosphere is overwhelmingly positive.

- Have a high degree of self-reliance. Family members have confidence that they can create successful families and that they can deal with whatever problems they encounter. When they do experience problems and crises, they have the ability to recover. Members of strong families can also accept help when they need it.

- Have close emotional connections. Members of strong families spend time together and do things together because they enjoy being with one another. They talk to one another and listen to one another, share everyday information, express positive feelings and appreciation, solve problems, and manage conflict productively.

- Have effective boundaries. Members of strong families respect each person and each role (husband, wife, parent, and child) in the family. They have the ability to be close and to allow family members to be individuals and to pursue personal goals. Family members respect one another as individuals and respect personal choices and personal freedom.

- Can adapt. Strong families are structured and predictable, but family members can make adjustments as they go through the lifecycle from becoming a couple, to becoming parents, launching children, growing up, and growing old. They can also adapt when they need to adjust to stressors such as illness, disability, deaths, job losses, and changes in the social and economic environment.

- Maintain effective gender relationships. People who create strong families honor both males and females, avoid letting gender stereotypes undermine their relationships, and create strong relationships between equals who respect and honor one another.

- Manage money effectively. Leaders in strong families usually share values about money and have a plan that helps them manage resources effectively. Strong families live within or below their means. Generally, members of strong families do not have to spend a lot of money and buy a lot of things to be happy. They avoid unnecessary debt and make a point of saving money for emergencies, and preparing for retirement.

- Meet the emotional, financial, educational, and spiritual needs of all family members. Members of strong families are committed to creating a healthy and satisfying lifestyle for every family member—children and adults including elderly family members.

- Share the burdens of life. There is no one way that responsibilities have to be divided, but in healthy families they are shared fairly and equitably. The unique abilities and talents of each family member are utilized. Each member is also willing to serve and to make sacrifices for the family when needed. Even children contribute.

- Have a strong support system. Members of strong families support one another and usually have the support of extended family members and friends, and have positive relationships with friends, neighbors, and community members.

- Develop and utilize the skills they need to create strong and satisfying marital and family relationships, and to be effective parents.

Points to Remember

- Religion and family are our oldest and most sacred institutions. Every society throughout history has had families and has practiced some kind of religion.
- Institutions are organized systems of behavior that help us meet a variety of our most basic and complex human needs.
- Our religion can provide valuable resources for strengthening families. The people whose marriages and families benefit the most from their religion have a deep internal faith, apply their beliefs to their marriages and family relationships, and attend a church.
- The most important core elements of our religion that can help families include faith, hope, love, grace, parenthood of God, forgiveness, and reconciliation.
- Happy marriages and strong families are important to adults and children, as well as society.
- All happy marriages and strong families are not exactly alike, but they have numerous shared characteristics.

Affirmations

- The Spirit of God guides me as I create strong relationships.
- I am totally committed to my family.
- I am creating a healthy family with Christian thoughts, feelings, intentions, and behaviors.

Helpful Activities

Please rate the degree to which you apply each of the following religious concepts or values to your relationships with <u>1</u> indicating the lowest degree (little or none) and <u>5</u> representing the highest degree (a lot). If you are married rate the questions in terms of your marriage and nuclear family. If you are not married, rate them in terms of your significant relationship or your relationship with members of your family of origin.

1 2 3 4 5   I am totally committed to my family.

1 2 3 4 5   I take responsibility for everything that happens in my family (or relationship).

1 2 3 4 5   I am generous to my (spouse and other) family members.

1 2 3 4 5   I am a caring (spouse and) family member.

1 2 3 4 5   I give and serve in my family.

1 2 3 4 5   I believe marriage and family are sacred institutions.

1 2 3 4 5   I participate in a church that values marriages and families and helps me succeed.

1 2 3 4 5   My religion helps me succeed in my (marriage and) family relationships.

1 2 3 4 5   I do my best to practice my beliefs and values in my family every day.

1 2 3 4 5   I accept my family members as they are rather than trying to change them.

1 2 3 4 5   I forgive my family members when they make mistakes.

1 2 3 4 5   I make up easily after a problem or conflict.

1 2 3 4 5   I believe my family members are important and worthwhile.

1 2 3 4 5   I love and respect my family members because we are all God's children.

1 2 3 4 5   I do not hold grudges when my family

members disappoint me.

There is no single established standard for scoring the instrument above, but higher scores are better than lower scores. We would expect that members of strong families would make an average of 4 which would be a total of 60 or higher. You might also use this scale to identify your most important strengths and any areas of weakness that can be improved. Probably any rating below 4 indicates an area where growth is needed.

Do not overlook opportunities to keep growing and build on strengths. You can develop areas where you identified a 4 to a 5. Of course, any scores of three or below are areas that need growth.

If you identify areas that need growth, also identify core elements of your religion that can help you grow in those categories and begin practicing them to increase the strengths of your family.

Please list the aspects of the relationships that you have identified as needing improvement and develop a plan for how to apply your religion/values to improve them and begin practicing now.

Notes

The discussion of religion and family, including the discussion of elements of religion that benefit families most, is based on my own research on the relationship between religion and family. See note for Brigman, *Religion and Family Strengths: An Approach to Wellness,* 1992, and Brigman, *Religion and Family Strengths: Implications for Mental Health Professionals,* 1992.

The discussion of who benefits most is based on a study I conducted using the Committed-Nominal Religious Attitude

Scale developed by Roger A. Meyer, PhD. This scale was designed to measure religious attitudes in six categories. My study indicated significant relationships between family strengths variables and one category of religious attitudes, *True Commitment*. See reference for Brigman and Keating, 1996.

In the discussion of family strengths, I have tried to summarize what I know about strong families and is based on the findings of many family strengths researchers. I acknowledge the contributions of these people.

CHAPTER 3

CREATING RELATIONSHIPS

Religion is an important thread in the fabric of our relationships. Its many fibers, such as faith, hope, love, and forgiveness, influence every aspect of our relationships.

Most of us could name a few major events that we think have shaped our lives: marriages, having children, divorces, and economic successes or failures. Most people believe that whether they succeed in their families will depend on how well they communicate, how well they manage conflict, or whether they marry the right persons.

The most important factors determining the quality of our relationships are tiny thoughts, feelings, intentions, and behaviors. Individually these little thoughts, feelings, intentions, and behaviors may not seem important. But they are the threads we weave into our lives and relationships. The quality of our relationships is based on the content of the fibers and the pattern we follow as we weave them.

We are always constructing, maintaining, or de-constructing our relationships with our thoughts, feelings, intentions, and behaviors. Here is how the process works.

If my wife is in a grouchy mood and says something I think is unkind, I have to decide how I am going to respond. My response will begin with my perception, or the way I understand the situation (thoughts). This perception will influence my feelings, my intentions, and my behavior. Then, my behavior will affect her behavior.

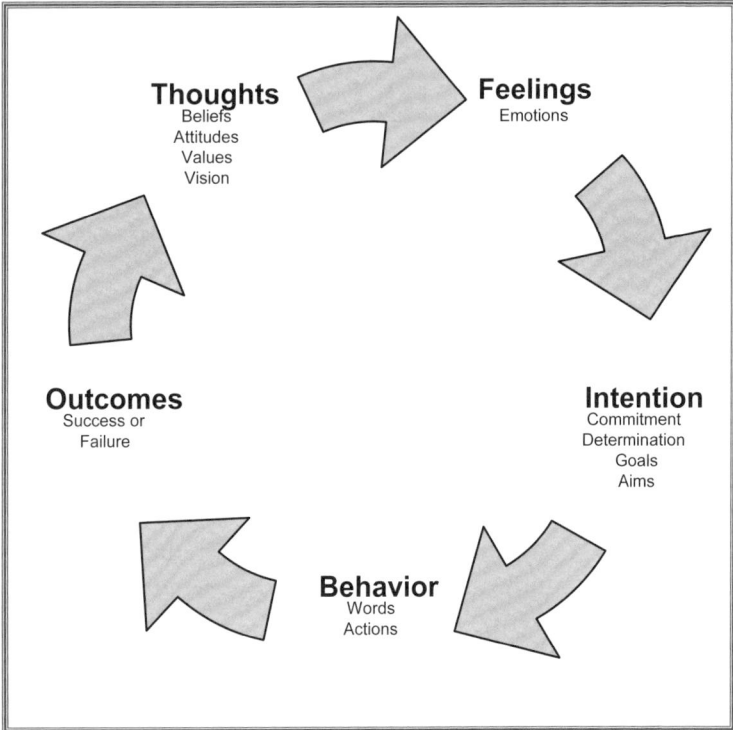

Consider the following three scenarios. Notice how thoughts (attitudes) influence the entire cycle. Also, notice that if I change any part of the cycle, I will change my own behavior, my wife's response, and our relationship.

First Scenario
Thoughts:	"She's being hateful."
Feelings:	Angry.
Thoughts:	"I can't let her get away with treating me this way."
Intentions:	To get even or at least make sure she

	doesn't treat me this way again.
Behaviors:	React with something grouchy such as, "Get off my back and leave me alone!" I may withdraw emotionally to reject her, or punish her. (I will probably tell myself that I am only protecting myself.)
Outcomes:	My behavior will make the problem worse and damage the relationship because it is unkind.

My response to my wife was based on my perception. That she yelled at me was a fact; that she was being hateful was only my perception.

My response was also based on the common notion that relationships depend on what others do. I did not think I was not responsible for the problem; I only did what I did because of what she did first. My problem was having a grouchy wife. The only way to solve the problem was to get my wife to change.

My response to my wife's yelling at me was also based on the principle of "an eye for an eye and a tooth for a tooth." She acted out of anger, and I got even by responding with anger. I thought she was being hateful to me and I repaid her with hatefulness. I got even, but each time I got even my behavior reduced the relationship to a lower level of functioning.

No one can expect to do what I did in this scenario and create a close and loving relationship anymore than we can expect to put cornbread in the oven and take out cake. If we want to make cake, we need to use flour instead of corn meal, and add some sugar.

Second Scenario

Thoughts:	"She's not being very thoughtful."
Feelings:	Annoyed.
Intentions:	Let her know this bothers me and try to

	help her understand what would work better.
Behaviors:	Tell her that her behavior is annoying me; make a suggestion about what would work better. For example, "I wish you'd talk more softly when you're angry," or "It really makes me sad when you yell at me, because then I feel unloved."
Outcomes:	My wife will probably consider my suggestions because they are reasonable and they were made appropriately. This kind of behavior usually maintains relationships.

This scenario is like the way many professionals teach us to deal with problems: when you have a problem, identify it, express your feelings, and negotiate a solution.

Every marriage requires some communication, expression of feelings, and negotiation. But communication does not solve problems. It is only a tool that lets people talk about problems. Expressing feelings can also be manipulative. When I tell my wife, "It really hurts me when you yell at me, because I do not feel like you love me," I expect her to quit yelling at me ("if she loves me," of course). If she yells at me again, then I will really feel unloved. I am holding her responsible for my feelings. Expressing my feelings also keeps me focused on my feelings instead of my goals.

Negotiation is a way that people try to talk others into changing. Even though I might offer to change something in return, my wife's knowing that I want to change her sends a message that I do not accept her the way she is.

No matter how much couples communicate, negotiate, and express their feelings, they will not be able to solve their problems until they learn to accept one another, forgive one another, and reconcile when they make mistakes.

The approach to solving problems used in the second scenario requires two people. This means husbands and wives think they cannot solve problems unless they both participate in the process and come to an agreement about a solution. This approach may leave both partners feeling helpless because each thinks the other partner is the only one who can solve the problem.

Third Scenario

Thoughts:	"She is being grumpy, she must have had a tough day."
Feelings:	Annoyed but compassionate. I care about her wellbeing. (I also understand what it is like to have a tough day).
Thoughts:	"She needs my support."
Intentions:	Be patient, caring, and supportive.
Behaviors:	Give her a hug and suggest, "You must have had a tough day. Is there anything I can do to help?"
Outcomes:	The relationship will be stronger and more satisfying. My behavior will help her deal with her frustrations and she will probably respond with kindness when I need support and someone to care.

This scenario is a good illustration of seeing a problem through eyes of faith and love and responding with Christian attitudes. It is also a good illustration of taking responsibility for being a loving spouse and creating a successful marriage. Notice that I acted lovingly even in a situation that could have been a cause of conflict. I was compassionate because I cared more about my wife's wellbeing than I cared about being right, winning, or getting my own way.

I realize that my wife's loving me does not mean that she will always be in a good mood or that she thinks I'm always

right or that she will always give in or that she does not have
preferences of her own. Even the most loving husbands and
wives have honest disagreements and personality differences.
We all have down days. When we accept our spouses by
grace, we accept them for who they are without trying to
change them.

When people who apply the core elements of their religion
in their marriages and families make decisions about their
lives and their impact on others, they consider whether their
behavior is kind, accepting, and forgiving.

For instance, if I follow my faith when my wife says
something grouchy, I will try to respond with kindness
because my religion teaches me to love compassionately and
to care about my wife's wellbeing. Eventually, she may have
less need to be grouchy because she feels loved and accepted.
If she does not quit being grouchy, I can still keep trying.

Creating Christian Relationships

Thoughts:	Perceive with eyes of faith.
Feelings:	Feel with loving hearts
Intentions:	To do what is right and good, kind and loving.
Behaviors:	Act with loving kindness.

The approach used in the third scenario is empowering. A
solution only requires one person, me. I can be the solution.
When my wife is angry, I can respond lovingly.

*One of the most damaging myths of marriage is that it
takes two people to solve a problem.*

In each instance, I had choices to make, and what I thought
set off a whole chain of events. The outcome of each approach

was different and ranged from damaging the relationship to strengthening it. The first scenario leads to failure, the second to a survival mode, and the third to marital success. Notice that my wife's behavior was exactly the same in each scenario. What I did made all the difference.

Resources for Growth: Changing the Patterns

"Do not conform yourself to this age but be transformed by the renewal of your mind, that you may discern what is the will of God, what is good and pleasing and perfect."

- Rom 12:2 NAB

As we begin our journey toward creating happy marriages and successful families, we need to be aware of the resources we have available to help us. As surprising as it may see, our genes and our memories are among the most important resources we have. A Christian approach to managing conflict is also vital for creating happy marriages and strong families.

Transforming Our Minds

My minister began his Pentecost sermon by asking how many of us believed we could make radical changes in our lives. Almost every hand in the congregation went up. Of course, we believe we can change. After all, the Bible teaches us we can be transformed by the renewing of our minds.

I have believed this concept of transformation all my life, but only recently have neuroscientists learned that when we change our minds, our brains literally change too.

Our brains are like muscles. When we give up old patterns

of thinking and behaving, the neural structures that supported them will atrophy like muscles that are not being used. When we begin using new patterns of thinking and behaving the neural structures we need to support them become larger and stronger.

For instance, a study of taxi drivers in London a few years ago showed that the hippocampus, the part of the brain that deals with spatial relationships, was much larger in the taxi drivers than in average people. Taxi drivers have to think about how to get to a destination and get there as quickly as possible, so the part of their brains they had to use the most actually enlarged.

Think about the implications of these findings for creating happy marriages and strong families. When we give up negative thoughts and feelings such as anger, envy, and resentment, the neural structures that supported those attitudes and behaviors shrink. When we begin loving compassionately, serving others, accepting our loved ones the way God made them, and forgiving them when they make mistakes, the neural structures we need to support these Christian virtues are strengthened. Thoughts, feelings, intentions, and behaviors that were once difficult can become natural for us.

One of the reasons I recommend Bible study, prayer, meditation, and affirmations for strengthening families is that every time we read a scripture, say a prayer, meditate, or affirm that with God's help we can create successful families, a whole new world unfolds in our brains that helps us create the happy marriages and strong families that we desire.

To be helpful, prayers, affirmations, meditation, and behavioral rehearsal must be based on our own behaviors rather than expectations for other people's behaviors. Time spent in spiritual activities is most useful when we are willing to do our part.

Our faith is creating our marriages when we feel angry or hurt and choose to be kind, patient, and forgiving.

Genes and Memories

Our genes and memories are important resources for transformation. We are bundles of genetic potentials. Our genetic blueprint is like a design portfolio – a group of possible lives we can build. We have genes that support our present behaviors and lifestyles; we have genes that will support other behaviors and lifestyles as well.

We have all known people who changed so dramatically that they seemed to be completely different. We have also known people whose transformation was a gradual process of growth, but who were none the less transformed.

When we begin trying to change our lives and relationships, we can find the new abilities we need to achieve our new goals because we have the genetic resources we need to support a variety of behaviors and lifestyles.

We all have an array of positive and negative memories. Most of us even have some traumatic memories that can weaken us or strengthen us. We can think of our memories as photos in the family album—a few shots that were taken at particular points in time.

Did you ever wonder why you remember some events in your life and seem to forget others? According to Psycho-theorist Alfred Adler, the memories we have stored in our family albums are memories of experiences we have chosen to remember because they will help us accomplish the goals we are pursuing or goals we are planning for the future. For instance, a person with a goal of staying safe at all costs might hold on to traumatic memories that will make him or her afraid to take risks. On the other hand, a person who has a goal of becoming a successful investor might hold on to memories about times when he or she had taken calculated risks in the past because such memories could help him or her have the courage to take the economic risks needed to make effective decisions about investments.

When we develop an intention to change our lives or relationships, our minds begin reviewing our memory banks looking for memories that can provide the resources we need. We have all had experiences when we needed to do something new, something out of our comfort zones. We often say something like, "I think I can do that. I remember when. . . ." When we do that, our minds are seeking memory resources to help us deal with a new challenge.

When we need to deal with challenges, we can revive positive memories that we have ceased to be aware of, or we can reevaluate our current memories and see our past events in more productive ways. For instance, instead of seeing how scared I was, I might notice how strong I was. Or I may become aware that even though an event was scary, God was there with me.

We can always update our photo albums. We can look for memories or focus on the parts of memories that will help us achieve our goals for family success. We can look for memories that can give us courage, strength, or patience.

According to Adler, when we change our goals, the memories in our family albums will also change.

No one has a single genetic blueprint; no one is destined by past experiences alone.

Whatever our genetic endowments or past experiences, we are creating our lives with our present thoughts, feelings, intentions, and behaviors.

Remember, our faith teaches us that we can be transformed by the renewing of our minds and that we can do all things through Christ who gives us strength. Our genes and memories are important resources for transformation.

Christian Conflict Skills

All families have to deal with conflict. More than anything else, how well families can deal with conflict will determine whether they succeed or fail. Most people can create successful relationships by following a Christian pattern of conflict resolution. When you need to deal with conflict

- Ask, "Is this conflict necessary?" "Will it be useful?" If not, forgive and let go.
- Recognize the position of the other person and acknowledge that you understand his or her point of view and his or her needs.
- Recognize that the other person is a child of God and has a right to his or her own preferences. Remember, you are your brother's keeper (not your brother's master).
- Focus on facts rather than on personalities or feelings. Avoid judgments.
- Be aware that if your family member is acting angrily or being unkind it is probably because he or she is afraid. Respond with love.
- Give gifts of the spirit – acceptance, understanding, compassion, respect, honor, forgiveness, and reconciliation.
- Ask the Spirit for guidance. "Holy Spirit, help me now" or affirm "The Spirit of God is with me as I resolve this conflict."
- Remember when you need to be right, to win, to get your own way, or to be served, you are not being led by the Spirit.
- Focus on solving your loved one's problem rather than having your own way.
- Give all you can first.
- Do not ask the family member to change.

- Focus on what you can do. You can ask yourself these questions: "What can I do?" "Will this work?" "Will this help?" "What else could I do?"
- Remember, communicating allows us to talk about problems, but only faith and hope, love and acceptance (grace), honor and respect (parenthood of God), and forgiveness and reconciliation can solve problems.

Conclusion

We can transform our lives and relationships when we give up limiting and unworkable beliefs about our lives and relationships and replace them with beliefs and attitudes such as faith and hope, love and grace, parenthood of God, and forgiveness and reconciliation that do work.

Whether we begin living according to Christian values early in life or later in life, our lives and our families can be shaped by the core elements of the Christian religion.

When we use our core values, we perceive through eyes of faith, feel with loving hearts, develop goals to do what is right and good, and act with loving kindness.

Our husbands and wives are the neighbors we are to love as ourselves, the brothers of whom we are keeper, and the brothers whom we are to forgive seventy times seven times.

Points to Remember

- We are always constructing, maintaining, or deconstructing our relationships with our thoughts, feelings, intentions, and behaviors.

- We can transform our lives by changing our minds (thoughts) which will lead to changed feelings, intentions, and behaviors.
- We have genes and memories of past events to support our current lives or different lives. When we develop an intention we can find the genes and memories that will give us the resources we need to carry them out.
- A Christian pattern of conflict can help us create happy marriages and strong families.

Affirmations

- The Spirit of God is helping me transform my life by changing the way I think, and I am thankful.
- The Spirit of God guides me as I create successful relationships.
- The Spirit of God is guiding me as I resolve this conflict, and I am thankful.
- I am a good forgiver.
- I always act lovingly no matter what others do.
- The Spirit of God is guiding me as I become a more patient husband or wife, and I am thankful.

Helpful Exercises

1. Think about your relationship goals and then write a brief statement that describes what you want to achieve.

2. Think about a recent incident that turned out really well. What was the outcome?

3. Now analyze your part of the process that led to that outcome.

    Thoughts:

    Feelings:

    Intentions:

    Behaviors:

4. What did you do to produce that outcome? How can you apply this success to other situations?

5. Identify a recent incident in a relationship that you thought resulted in a problem. What was the outcome?

6. Now analyze the process that led to that outcome.

    Thoughts:

    Feelings:

    Intentions:

    Behaviors:

7. What did you do to produce that outcome?

8. What could you change that might turn this problem to a positive outcome that will help you reach your relationship goal?

9. Analyze a memory that has had a limiting effect on your life. What can you learn about yourself from this memory? How can it be a sense of strength and growth for you?

Notes

Discussion of the Adlerian theory is based on Dreikurs, Rudolf R. *Fundamentals of Adlerian Psychology.* Chicago: Alfred Adler Institute, 1950.

For a succinct discussion of neuroscience, see N. T. Wright, pp. 37-43. Also see *Brain Rules* by John Medina. Seattle: Pear Press, 2008, pp. 58-62. This information is also available in a variety of recent articles and books about the findings of modern neuroscience.

CHAPTER 4

AS LONG AS WE BOTH
SHALL LIVE

"A simple but, we believe, true answer to the question of why marriage is in trouble is that Americans have invested less moral, spiritual, cultural, political, and legal energy into supporting the marriage vow."

- Linda Waite and Maggie Gallagher, *The Case for Marriage*, p. 176.

After spending most of her professional life studying marriages and families, in *The Good Marriage: How and Why Love Lasts,* psychologist Judith Wallerstein wrote, "As our fiftieth wedding anniversary approaches, I have thought long and hard about what my husband and I have done to protect our marriage. Why we have been able to love each other for so many years? . . . What have I learned that I can pass on to my children and grandchildren?" (p. 8).

She goes on to reason: "I certainly have not been happy all through each year of my marriage. There have been good times and bad, angry and joyful moments, times of ecstasy and times of quiet contentment" (p.8).

Then she gives us the secret of her success: she made a choice and she stuck with it. "I would never trade my husband,

Robert, for another man," she said. "I would not swap my marriage for any other. This does not mean that I find other men unattractive, but there is all the difference in the world between a passing fancy and a life plan. For me, there has been only one life plan, the one I have lived with my husband" (p. 8).

Yes, Dr. Wallerstein's marriage lasted through the good times and the bad times because she had made an unwavering commitment to stay married, but even more importantly, she had made a commitment to honor her husband, her marriage, and their life together.

Commitment is the foundation that supports every other aspect of successful marriages and strong families. When husbands and wives are unwaveringly committed, their commitment influences every thought, feeling, and behavior.

Supports for Marriage

> An attitude of grace can help us replace no-fault divorces with no-fault marriages.

The lives of people who are married are totally entwined. The relationship links them together emotionally, but getting married ties them together legally, financially, and socially. Having children links parents together for the rest of their lives.

Whether we succeed or fail in our families depends more than anything else on how well we are able to keep our commitments. We need all the support we can get. The legal contract, religious covenant, and the support of a community of friends and family all help provide structure and support for marriages and families.

The Legal Marriage: The Contract

The process of getting married begins at the court house when the bride and groom get the marriage license. When they affirm their intent to be married by saying "I do" before witnesses and a judge, justice of the peace, or a religious leader who signs the marriage license, they will be married.

Marriage is a contract between the bride and groom and the state. Getting married changes a romance into a lifestyle complete with a legal identity. In effect, marriage creates a corporation that allows couples to combine their lives, their assets, their resources, and their futures.

Historically, once people were legally married the contract could be dissolved only if one of the partners had violated the marriage in some serious way such as adultery or desertion.

Deterrents to divorce can actually help people succeed because for marriages to be happy, they first have to be secure. Since the advent of no-fault divorce in the 1960s, some of the protective functions of the marriage contract have been reduced because under no-fault divorce laws, either spouse has the right to have a divorce.

Getting married makes relationships stronger and more stable. Once people are married they cannot just get angry and walk out. Ending a marriage is complicated, expensive, and takes time. The effects of divorce are sweeping and traumatic; it dissolves the corporation and people's identity and social status along with it. The marriage contract provides stability and structure for marriage, but little real holding power.

"The weakening of marriage is the most important social problem facing America today."   - James Q. Wilson, *What Is America's Most Serious Social Problem?*

The Religious Marriage: The Covenant

Most Christians want to be married in a church, or at least in a religious ceremony. They promise before God and witnesses that they will love, cherish, and honor one another for as long "as we both shall live." Most Christians would agree that their vows create a covenant between themselves and God.

In our society, most contracts are based on written agreements that are signed and notarized. But we still follow the practice of taking vows in the name of God in two important situations: when we promise to tell the truth when we testify in court, and when we promise to keep our marriage vows as long as we both shall live.

The concept of covenant has its roots in the Old Testament. In Old Testament times important agreements were sealed by taking a vow in the name of God. When people made agreements in the name of God, they were expected to keep their promises no matter what. Breaking a promise made in the name of God was taking God's name in vain.

Covenants are stronger than contracts. One way to understand the difference between a contract and a covenant is that prenuptial agreements are contracts. They are about property: what belongs to whom, and what will happen to assets based on events and circumstances such as death or divorce.

Covenants are not contingent on events or behaviors. Even though marriage vows acknowledge that the couple will have to deal with events and circumstances such as "sickness and health," and "for better" and "for worse," the people who take the vows still promise to love one another, cherish and honor one another, and be faithful to one another for the remainder of their lives – no matter what.

Most Christians would agree that husbands and wives should not consider ending their marriages unless they experience severe problems that cannot be resolved such as domestic violence, infidelity, severe emotional abuse, or criminal behavior. Or, if one of the partners leaves and will not consider reconciling.

Traditionally, the marital covenant has had strong support from churches. Churches expected people who got married to remain married for the rest of their lives.

Today churches may not have as much power as they had in the past. But they still have a lot of influence, especially when they have a reverence for marriage and family as sacred institutions and openly support them. People are looking for leadership from their churches.

Some examples of teachings from the Bible that support families are "Thou shalt not commit adultery." "Thou shalt not covet thy neighbor's wife." "Husbands, love your wives as Christ loves the church." "Wives respect your husbands." "Children, obey your parents." "Fathers, provoke not your children to wrath." And, injunctions discouraging divorce and violence.

The Social Marriage

In *The Case for Marriage,* Linda Waite and Maggie Gallagher say, "Marriage is what lovers do when they want to bring their love out of the merely private, internal realm of emotion and make it a social fact, something visible to and acknowledged by everybody from parents to bank clerks" (p. 18).

Getting married creates a clear status that is recognized by friends, family members, and society in general. We know how to treat people who are married, and marriages are generally valued and supported in our society.

Getting married also helps people develop a support group

of other married couples. People usually fit into and are welcomed by groups of other people like themselves. Married people can increase their chances of success by associating with other people who value their marriages and are succeeding.

> *Believing we can associate with negative people and not be*
> *affected by their attitudes is like believing we can*
> *swim in a polluted lake without being contaminated.*

The Personal Commitment

The legal, moral, religious, and social aspects of commitment all provide support for marriage and a deterrent to divorce. But these alone cannot guarantee success. We must add our own personal determination to create a successful marriage. Keeping a commitment to life-long marriage is a process that we need to follow every day in many little ways. We must be willing to do whatever it takes to succeed—even when it is hard.

How to Honor Our Commitments

Attitudes are expectations about life that we make come true.

Successful couples take responsibility for their marriages. Their success is not determined by things that happen to them, but by the decisions they make. It is not their love that holds their relationship together, but their commitment to one another that holds their love together.
   - Brigman, *Marriage: A Simple Guide to Success,* p. 21.

Succeeding in marriage is like going to school. Graduation is the goal. But we achieve it one day at a time, one course at a time, one paper at a time, and one exam at a time. We succeed when we stay focused during the easy times and when we try hardest when it is most difficult.

An unwavering commitment to marriage begins with an intention to stay married and, even more importantly, a commitment to the process of doing what is required to succeed day by day and moment by moment. To be effective our goals need to be for ourselves and need to contain things not to do, such as, "I will not lose my temper and say unkind words when I am angry" or "I will not withdraw emotionally when I get my feelings hurt," but mostly things to do, such as, "I will accept my spouse as he or she is, tolerate his or her weaknesses, and forgive his or her mistakes."

When couples are drowning in marital problems, they notice the big things such as how much they fight, how much they have been hurt by one another, and how bad they feel. But their conflicts, differences, and hurt feelings are the results of their problems, not the causes. The real problems are the little thoughts and attitudes, feelings, and behaviors that caused the conflicts and hurt feelings.

A small resentment in a marriage is like a drop of black ink in a glass of clear water.

Unfortunately, marriages are already failing by the time most people realize they have serious problems. Failure is a process just as success is a process.

Marriages began to break down when husbands and wives
- Lose sight of their goal and begin taking their marriages and their partners for granted. Athletes call this losing concentration.
- Overlook opportunities to build relationships. They may quit loving and cherishing, just a little bit at first,

then more later.

- Have a problem and let themselves feel anger and hold little resentments. People who hold even the smallest resentments begin feeling emotionally distant.
- Begin blaming one another. Once problems are the spouse's fault people can no longer fix them; they can only fight about them.
- Begin believing their way is right, and especially when they begin believing their spouses are wrong and need to change.
- Begin expressing open conflict. Hateful words and deeds said or done in moments of anger can have long-lasting effects.
- Dwell on fantasies about how they might have a better relationship with another person. When they let themselves begin to wonder they are getting all they deserve out of their marriages.
- Begin wondering whether they should stay and, particularly, when they let themselves begin to wonder whether they should leave.

People who fantasize about other relationships are involved in a love triangle with a fantasy that their spouses can never live up to.

Successful couples create their successes step by step starting with little thoughts and attitudes that lead to feelings, and behaviors. They are compassionate, accepting, and forgiving during good times and bad times alike.

People who have an unwavering commitment for their families let their goals determine their behavior instead of reacting to events and circumstances. When they encounter problems, they find solutions. When the going gets tough, they try harder.

Successful husbands and wives choose to see the best in one another and their relationships, and choose to have

positive feelings about one another, their marriages and
families even in tough times. They consciously make
decisions to engage in positive behaviors that lead to success
even in moments when they are feeling hurt or angry.

Successful husbands and wives do not spend time
wondering whether they married the right person, whether
they should stay married, whether they are happy, or whether
they might be happier in another relationship. This kind of
evaluation creates unhappiness and weakens the whole family.

Successful husbands and wives take advantage of
opportunities to be thoughtful, to express appreciation, and to
engage in acts of kindness. When something does not work,
successful husbands and wives try something else until they
find something that does work.

When they have a problem, husbands and wives who
create successful marriages choose to work together as
partners instead of becoming opponents and blaming. When
they have a disagreement, they ask what they can do instead of
defending themselves. They tolerate and compensate for one
another's weaknesses. They accept their spouses as they are,
forgive them when they make mistakes, and stay connected
even when they are tempted to withdraw emotionally. They
take responsibility for being the best husbands and wives they
can be.

Concluding Remarks

Failure is easy; anyone can do it. Success is a choice that
usually requires skill and effort.

The Christian concepts taught in this chapter can be
utilized to create a new relationship, improve an already good
relationship, or revitalize a relationship that is in trouble. They
seem highly idealistic, and they are. But faith and hope, love
and grace, honor and respect (parenthood of God), forgiveness
and reconciliation are the tools of the Spirit, and they work.

The challenges we face in our marriages can be opportunities to fight about our differences or opportunities to love one another the way God loves.

People who express their commitment in little ways over and over as they go through life have no difficulty remaining married, staying in love, and being happy for a whole lifetime.

Many successful couples have made commitments that have carried them through fifty, sixty, and even seventy years of marriage.

One day while I was writing at McDonalds, an elderly man came up to me and asked, "What cha writing?"

"A book," I said.

"What about?"

"Marriage."

"I know a lot about marriage," he said; "I've been married for 67 years."

The elderly gentleman went on to tell me that his wife was ill. He had been taking care of her at home for the past few years. But recently her needs had become so great that she had to go to a nursing home. Now he visits her every day, he told me. But, he confessed that he does not think she recognizes him any more.

So, why does he keep visiting her if she no longer recognizes him? I suspect he visits her in the nursing home every day because he recognizes her. She is the woman he loves. The woman who has been his friend, partner, and lover for 67 years. And, the woman he promised to take care of "in sickness and in health," and "for as long as you both shall live."

By spending time with her every day, he can make sure she is being treated well and that her needs are being met. And, perhaps she will not be as lonely if he holds her hand.

The elderly gentleman was just an ordinary guy. He had probably never read a book or taken a course about marriage.

But he knew what it takes to succeed in marriage is pretty basic. Always honor your commitments, do your best, keep trying, be kind and loving, forgive your loved ones when they mess up.

This man is not a rare example. More than half of all marriages last for a lifetime. Many men and women help one another through their later years. It is a promise they made to one another when they got married, and it is a promise they can keep.

In *Marriage and Snow on the Mountain*, Joseph Sittler says, "The heart of marriage is a promise. . . . I'm really challenged toward fulfillment only when I understand marriage as a mutual acceptance of a challenge to fulfill the seemingly impossible. Then there is something that is really worth the human effort" (p. 17).

Points to Remember

- Successful marriages are based on a strong commitment which for Christians is often considered a covenant between themselves and God.
- A covenant recognizes problems and contingencies but is intended to be kept no matter what.
- People who succeed in keeping their covenants are committed to the process of doing what is required to succeed day by day and moment by moment.
- To be effective our goals need to be for ourselves and need to contain things not to do such as, "I will not lose my temper and say unkind words when I am angry," or "I will not withdraw emotionally when I get my feelings hurt," but mostly things to do such as, "I will accept my spouse as he or she is, tolerate his or her weaknesses, and forgive his or her mistakes."
- The most successful people apply the core Christian concepts of faith and hope, love and grace, respect and

honor, and forgiveness and reconciliation to every step of the process.

Affirmations

- I always keep my commitments to my spouse and family.
- The Spirit of God guides me as I honor my promises to my family every day and every moment.
- With God's help I always do my best to be a good husband or wife.

Helpful Exercises

1. If you are married, try to remember what you promised when you got married. Make a list of the things you covenanted to do in your marriage. Then rate how well you are doing on each one on a scale of 1 (lowest degree) to 5 (highest degree). Here are some of the things that people typically promise to do: love, cherish, honor, be faithful, give ourselves sexually, communicate, solve problems, and remain committed in sickness and in health, for better or worse, and as long as they both live.

After you have made the list and rated how well you are doing in each category, develop a plan to work on any areas that need improvement.

2. If you are not married, write a set of marriage vows or a list of promises. You might begin this way, "I covenant with -_____ and with God to . . . . Then list what you are willing to promise.

What Supports will help most?

When you have completed your vows, discuss how you will keep your promises moment by moment in your marriage during good times and challenging times.

What spiritual resources will you need to be able to keep your promises?

Review your commitment to your family relationships. Does it reflect your spiritual beliefs?

3   Write a brief description of the kind of husband or wife you want to be. Then discuss whether your behavior is helping you be the kind of spouse you want to be or whether it is preparing you to be the kind of spouse you want to be

In what areas do you need to improve to help you accomplish your goals?

How can your religion help you accomplish your goals?

CHAPTER 5

A GRAIN OF MUSTARD SEED

"For truly I tell you, if you have faith the size of a mustard seed, you will say to this mountain, 'Move from here to there,' and it will move; and nothing will be impossible for you."

- Mathew 17:20

Whenever faith was mentioned in the little country church of my youth, someone would always define it by quoting Hebrews 11:1. The old King James Version says, "Faith is the substance of things hoped for, the evidence of things not seen." Then, someone always asked, "What does it mean?" The person quoting the verse would insist: "It means just what it says!" Everyone, including me, would agree. But I always wondered, "What did it say?"

Newer versions of the Bible have used words such as *assurance* and *conviction* instead of *substance* and *evidence* to make Hebrews 11:1 easier to understand. But, the words *substance* and *evidence* may help us understand faith and hope better.

At the simplest level, faith is a belief or pattern of beliefs. We believe in God and we have confidence in God's promises. Faith is the foundation that supports all other spiritual qualities such as love and grace and forgiveness and reconciliation. Faith is also an essential ingredient in every successful endeavor including successful families.

Hope is faith in expression. When we hope we anticipate the promised outcome and become actively involved in creating what we believe in and hope for. Through faith and hope we can create successful families because we believe our families are important, we believe that with God's help we can succeed, and we are willing to do our best.

We can think of faith as the artist's easel, canvas, paints, and brush. When the artist takes the brush in hand and starts putting the paints onto the canvas, she is expressing hope. Stroke by stroke as she applies the paints, she creates the image she had in her mind. Faith (believing it could be done and that she could do it) was her best evidence that she could create the image, and through hope (faith in expression) her faith becomes the painting (the substance of things hoped for).

Like the artist who applied the paints to the canvas, we can create successful families thought by thought, feeling by feeling, intention by intention, and behavior by behavior. As we apply faith and hope, love and grace, honor and respect, and forgiveness and reconciliation to our relationships we can create the happy marriages and strong families we desire, the substance of things hoped for.

Our faith influences what we believe about families, how we perceive our family members and their behavior, who we are, what we do, and what we believe we are capable of doing.

What We Believe: Faith in Marriage and Family

"Family relationships are ventures in faith. Faith influences the way people perceive life and can help them find meaning and purpose even in family difficulty."
- Brigman, *Dealing With Religion in Therapy*, p. 43.

When I was in seminary I was required to take two semesters of systematic theology. Seminarians study theology by reading the works of the great theologians just as students of philosophy read the writings of great philosophers. During those two semesters, the class read the works of theologians from St. Augustine and Thomas Aquinas to Martin Luther and John Calvin, as well as later theologians such as Tillich, Zwingly, Kierkegaard, and Barth.

Each of the great theologians helped us understand some aspect of our religion better. I especially appreciated Karl Barth. Barth helped me understand that God always has been and always is creating and redeeming. Even more importantly, Barth helped me understand that through our families we are partners with God in creation and redemption.

The long genealogies in the Bible are accounts of God's creation and redemption. Down in the country where I was raised, we called these the "begats" because in the old King James Version they went something like this: "Abraham begat Isaac, and Isaac begat Jacob, and Jacob begat. . . ," and on and on. "Why can't we just skip these boring lists," I often wondered, "and get down to the important stuff?"

Barth helped me understand that these genealogies are the important stuff. They show us that human families, such as Noah and his family, Abraham and Sarah, Isaac and Rebecca, and many other families have had important roles in creation and redemption.

The begats also show us that God uses ordinary people and ordinary families to accomplish extraordinary events. Families are so important that even Jesus needed to be raised in an ordinary human family.

Christians believe that the family is a sacred institution and parenthood is a sacred trust. Barth helped me understand how important our families – yours and mine - really are.

What kind of world we create is determined largely by the quality of families we create. Adults are psychologically and emotionally more stable, happier, and more productive when they live in close families. The family is by far the best structure for producing and rearing children, and for preparing them for responsible roles in society. It is in families that we learn our faith, our attitudes, our values, and the patterns by which we live our lives.

Christians know how important families are. And because of our faith, we believe we can create successful families.

How We See

"Do you see the man in the moon?" the father asks? "See it up there?" "See the eyes and the nose?"

"Oh, I see it now," the child replies.

"Can you find the big dipper?" "Look over there. See that star, and that one, and that one? Connect them together and they are shaped like a dipper."

"Oh, I see."

From that time on, whenever the child looks into the night sky she will see the man in the moon and the big dipper. This is how she has learned to organize and interpret the sky. She sees the man in the moon and the big dipper because that is the way she has learned to see.

One of the most profound teachings of Jesus is "If your eye is healthy, your whole body will be full of light; but if your eye is unhealthy, your whole body will be full of darkness" (Mathew 6:22-23).

Have you ever heard the expression, "I'll believe it when I see it?" For many years of my life, that was a common expression for me. But, I no longer say, "I'll believe it when I see it" because I have learned that we tend to see what we believe, and through seeing it that way we make it so - especially where relationships are concerned.

"People only see what they are prepared to see."
– Ralph Waldo Emerson

In college I read an article that illustrated how the teacher's perception of a student's behavior affected how he treated the student and how the student performed in the class. For instance, once a teacher believed that a student was uncooperative, a trouble maker, or a poor scholar, the teacher tended to "see" all the negative behaviors and overlook the positive behaviors. Eventually, he could only see the student as a problem.

When behavioral analysts came into the classroom and counted the behaviors the teacher had identified as problems, they often found that the identified behaviors did not occur nearly as often as the teacher had reported. They sometimes found that other students that had been identified as well-behaved engaged in the problem behaviors as often as or even more often than the student that had been identified as the "problem." What the teacher believed about the student affected which behaviors the teacher noticed and how he interpreted the meaning of these behaviors.

What the teacher believed about the student determined how he treated the student, how the student reacted, and ultimately how well the student did in the class. People – students, husbands, wives, parents, and children - tend to live up to (or down to) people's expectations of them.

In the movie *Fireproof* Caleb and Catherine are on the verge of divorce when Caleb's father suggests that Caleb try a faith-based approach to saving his marriage. This results in a radical change in Caleb's behavior. Instead of being arrogant and uncaring, Caleb begins being kind and helpful.

Catherine finds Caleb's new attitude confusing and tells a colleague at work that she does not understand what Caleb is trying to do. This colleague tells her about a cousin who had recently gotten a divorce. As they neared the divorce, her cousin's husband had begun being nice to her so he could get her to agree to a better settlement from the divorce. She tells Catherine she should be careful and not let Caleb do that to her. From that time on, Catherine begins to see Caleb's kind behaviors as an attempt to cheat her out of her fair share. Probably so he can keep the $20,000 he had saved to buy a new boat which Catherine thinks he loves more than he loves her anyway. Once Catherine believes Caleb is trying to cheat her, she can only see what she believes about Caleb. She sees evidence of his unkind motives in Caleb's every act of love.

The way Catherine saw Caleb determined how she treated him and the decisions she made about their marriages. Caleb's every kind behavior caused Catherine to became more determined to get a divorce.

What we believe about men, women, and marriage affects how we see our spouses and our marriages, how we interpret our partners' behavior, how we treat them, and how they respond. Our perceptions become our reality. Husbands and wives tend to live up to or down to their spouses' expectations.

As a society we are experiencing a crisis of faith in marriage and families. We tend to emphasize and exaggerate problems and overlook successes. A single incident of family violence may get national news coverage while countless millions of couples who are never violent (and most are not) go unnoticed. Divorces and family failures usually become public while couples who have loved, cherished, and honored one another for a lifetime go unmentioned. The high divorce rate makes headlines frequently, but the high marriage rate does not even make the news once a year. A few parenting failures get attention while millions of mothers and fathers who are doing a good job go unrecognized.

You must not lose faith in humanity. Humanity is an ocean; if a few drops of the ocean are dirty, the ocean does not become dirty.   – Mohandas Ghandi

Jesus taught us that faith is the healthy eye because we create what we believe (See). Couples who see life through eyes of faith can understand how important marriages and families are to men, women, children, and society. They believe they can succeed. And when they apply their faith and move forward with hope, they can.

Did You Know?

- More than half of all marriages last a lifetime and the majority of married people say they are happily married.
- Most parents are doing a good job and most children grow up healthy and productive.
- Most relationships are not violent and violence and the rate of spousal violence and abuse is lowest for couples who are married, and the lowest rate of child abuse is in families with two biological parents.
- Americans love marriage and almost everyone who can does get married. We have one of the highest marriage rates in the world.

Who We Are: Character

We generally think living a Christian life is about following a lot of rules - do not steal, cheat, lie, or commit adultery. But in his most scathing criticism, Jesus called the scribes and Pharisees "hypocrites" (Matthew 23:13), which means "actors." It seems that Jesus criticized the Scribes and Pharisees for living the Christian life as if they were playing a role or reading lines from a script. They were following the rules right out of the book, but Jesus wanted them (and us) to live the Christian life from their hearts. To live the Christian life from their hearts, their behavior needed to be an expression of Christian character.

What Is Character?

Character is who we are - all the features and traits that form our personalities and our nature. In *After You Believe: Why Christian Character Matters,* N. T. Wright says, "Human "character" . . . is the pattern of thinking and acting which runs right through someone, so that wherever you cut into them . . . you see the same person through and through (p. 27).

Character is like an orange. An orange looks orange. If you scrape off the skin, you get orange zest. If you peel it, you get orange fruit. If you squeeze it, you get orange juice. An orange is an orange inside and out.

When people live from character, they do not react to circumstances, events, or the behavior of other people. A person who has developed a loving character will think and act lovingly – no matter what others do. Like oranges, our lives and behavior are always an expression of character. We can only express what we are.

The first, and perhaps the most important, aspect of faith is that faith is the source of character. When we develop Christian character we become what we believe.

Character affects every aspect of our lives, even whom we marry. We naturally attract and are attracted to people who are a lot like us. People who have similar attitudes are often attracted to one another because they share many of the same goals and desire many of the same qualities about marriage and about life in general. People often say they were attracted to their partners because of their faith.

People who are best suited for marriage are mature, confident, optimistic, well adjusted, and ready for marriage. They are able to accept other people as they are, care about the needs of other people, and able to respect and get along with other people. They have a positive attitude. They can experience conflict without getting angry or holding grudges, make sacrifices when necessary, and forgive family members who make mistakes.

People who are impulsive, demanding, selfish, impatient, argumentative, critical, and slow to forgive, and those who do not have good relationship skills have difficulty creating happy relationships. Succeeding in relationships is particularly difficult for people who expect to win, to be right, to get their own way, or to be served.

When we have developed the kind of character that is suitable for being good husbands and wives, we will naturally do things that lead to happy marriages and strong families. When we develop Christian character, loving another person becomes more important than winning, being right, or getting our own way. Forgiveness becomes more important than being fair or getting even. Serving becomes more important than being served.

How We Develop Christian Character

> "The qualities of character which Jesus and his first followers insist on as the vital signs of healthy Christian life don't come about automatically. You have to develop them. You have to work at them. You have to think about it, to make conscious choices to allow the Holy Spirit to form your character in ways that, to begin with, seem awkward and "unnatural."
> - N. T. Wright, *After You Believe: Why Christian Character Matters,* pp. 27-28.

We develop Christian character when we open ourselves to the leadership of the Spirit, when we fill our minds with Christian principles by studying the Bible and other religious materials, when we spend time in prayer and meditation, and when we do affirmations about our faith.

> "The highest and best work of imagination is the marvelous transformation that it works in character. Imagine that you are one with the principal of good, and you will become truly good."   - Charles Fillmore, *The Unity Treasure Chest.*

Eventually, Christian thoughts, intentions, feelings, and behaviors, such as being kind, acting lovingly, accepting others, honoring our family members as children of God, and forgiving, can become natural. At that point we will not have to follow a script because the principles of our faith will have become part of our character.

What We Do: Faith in Expression

Basing a marriage on a quick romance is like driving a car off a cliff and expecting a smooth flight and a safe landing at the desired destination.

When I ran into Claudia in our minister's office, she told me she was there to make arrangements for her wedding. She explained that she and Germane had met about a month before. Their romance had developed quickly. "It's uncanny," she said. "We just have everything in common. We're soul mates."

Claudia and Germane believed they loved one another so much that their relationships would last forever. They decided to get married right away. A few weeks later I learned that the wedding had been called off.

Claudia and Germane had based their relationship on faulty ideas and romantic feelings. They were planning to get married without adequate evaluation or preparation. Fortunately, Claudia and her ever-so-brief fiancé found out they were not suited for one another before they got married.

It is foolishness to expect that we can behave recklessly and the Spirit will clean up the mess for us.

Evaluate

People who live by faith take responsibility for making good decisions. When they are considering marriage, they evaluate the relationship and base their decision to get married on clear evidence that marriage is right for them, that the time is right, and that they are ready to make a total commitment to the marriage and to their partners.

People who are considering marriage can evaluate whether their prospective mates are appropriate for them. They can also evaluate the strength of the relationship by asking, "Do I still love her when I'm angry or disappointed?" "Are his needs at least as important to me as my own needs and feelings?" and "Am I still committed to the relationship when things are not going well?" "Can we get along well enough to solve most of our problems?" "Can we adapt to most of our differences and cope with the rest of them?"

Dating and courtship are appropriate times for evaluation and decision-making about whether to get married. When people continue the evaluation and decision-making processes beyond the time they get married, they are doubting. Just as faith creates positive outcomes, doubt creates negative outcomes. No one can develop a happy marriage as long as he continues evaluating and deciding.

TIP: Whether you are in a relationship or already married it is important to avoid secret tests. An example of such a test is when one partner has scheduled an activity and the other partner wants to spend the time together. She might say, "It's ok. Go ahead and go with your friends; we can do something together later," when really she (or he) was thinking, "If he really loves me he will decide to spend the evening with me even if I tell him it's ok to go." Such tests are doomed for failure and are detrimental to relationships because they are dishonest and manipulative. Such behaviors can start a whole cycle of negativity in the relationship. If the event is important it would be best to be honest and say, "I really need you to do this with me." Be reasonable; not all events can be rescheduled, and no couple has a 100 percent agreement on schedules. It is neither partner's responsibility to be available at all times.

Prepare for Marriage

Adjustment to marriage requires husbands and wives to blend two sets of lifestyle patterns into a shared habit system that will work for them as a couple. Relationships work best when couples allow time to develop many of these shared lifestyles gradually before they get married. When they do this, they have established patterns they can use when they get married. When they do get married they can work together to develop patterns for dealing with the remaining challenges of married life together.

Couples need to learn how to solve problems together before they get married. When couples who have learned to solve problems together have a serious problem or conflict, they can be confident they can find a solution because they have resolved problems and conflicts together before.

What If You Are in a Troubled Marriage?

There are many strong and happy marriages, but some marriages do not meet the most basic physical and emotional needs of husbands and wives and other family members. A few marriages are abusive. Most troubled marriages are riddled with chronic conflict that the partners have been unable to deal with.

When marriages are failing, the choices people have are pretty simple: stay in the marriage the way it is, improve the marriage, or end the marriage.

If the marriage is violent or dangerous, people need to get help immediately, and do whatever is required to keep everyone in the family safe, even while they make decisions about whether to try to improve the relationship or end it. If the relationship is not dangerous or violent it is certainly in everyone's best interest to try to improve the relationship. Divorce can help people run from problems temporarily, but it seldom solves problems. And, divorce causes many other problems.

Most marriages can be revitalized. Most couples who meet, date, fall in love, and get married have ample similarities to develop happy marriages and strong families. If they did not, they would not have been attracted to one another and would not have been able to get a relationship started, much less carry it on long enough to fall in love, get engaged, and get married.

When couples start having problems they do not know how to manage, they often get scared. Their feelings of love get blocked by fear and can change to feelings of contempt. Then they begin blaming one another, defending themselves, and withdrawing emotionally.

The qualities that brought troubled couples together and helped them form their relationship in the first place are usually still there hidden under layers of anger, fear, and pain. If husbands and wives can get over their fears, the love can be revived.

If you want to revitalize a troubled relationship you can replace faulty patterns of interaction with behaviors that are based on spiritual principles. It only takes one person acting in faith to turn a relationship around.

When husbands or wives begin applying the tools of the Spirit they can replace fear and doubt with faith and hope, they can replace anger and rejection with love and grace, they can replace contempt with respect and honor, and they can replace holding grudges and withdrawing emotionally with forgiveness and reconciliation.

Successful couples do not necessarily have fewer problems than unsuccessful couples, but they deal with them differently. When couples who experience problems and crises are able to stick together and deal with their problems as a team, they grow closer. When couples encounter serious problems and react with fear and blame one another, their relationships will be torn apart.

Faith and Parenthood

"The best institutional friend that children have is marriage, and if grownups make a mess of it, the children are going to suffer"   - David Blankenhorn, quoted by Sharon Jayson.

Most Christian parents believe God gave them their children and that raising them is their most important responsibility.

A stable marriage is one of the most important gifts parents can give their children. On average, families with two biological parents do far better than any other family form. According to the National Council on Family Relations, the largest organization of family-life professionals in the United States, healthy married-parent families are the best environment for children. Children are safer and happier, and grow up to be more capable and productive when they are raised by their own two parents who are married to one another.

There is considerable evidence that divorce has serious detrimental affects on children for the rest of their lives. Children benefit a lot from an average family, or even a marginal family in most cases.

Most divorces today do not come from high conflict marriages. In many divorcing families the children are doing fine until their lives are torn apart by the divorce. Most divorces can be avoided no matter how troubled the relationship.

Where children are concerned, the professionals live in two worlds. On the one hand, our standards for rearing children are the highest they have ever been. It seems parents cannot do enough or be perfect enough for their children. On the other hand, despite mounds of research indicating that two-parent families are important for children's wellbeing, it is not popular to say anything about the importance of family structure. Parents can walk away from their parental commitments without much social stigma. Even though our culture has produced several generations of war-torn marriages and battle-scarred youth, it is not politically correct to suggest parents should commit themselves to making a home for their children.

A Final Story

"Whatever course you decide upon, there is always someone to tell you that you are wrong. There are always difficulties arising which tempt you to believe that your critics are right. To map out a course of action and follow it to an end requires courage."   - Ralph Waldo Emerson.

As children, most of us were inspired by *The Little Engine That Could*. This book is about a little engine that needed to pull a train over a high mountain to deliver toys and food to children on the other side. To succeed the little engine had to believe it could climb the mountain and be willing to put all its effort and energy into making it to the top.

The most vivid image most of us have of this story is the little engine saying, "I think I can, I think I can, I think I can" as it chugged up the mountain.

The story of *The Little Engine That Could* is about faith and hope. The little engine believed that climbing the mountain was important and that it could do it. That was faith. When the little engine put all its effort and energy into climbing the mountain, that was hope. By putting faith into action the little engine created the success it had hoped for.

Our faith teaches us that with God's help, we can do all things. That includes creating happy marriages and strong families, being good husbands and wives, and being good mothers and fathers.

Successful relationships require courage. The best source of courage is our faith.

It is never too late to begin learning how to apply spiritual principles to our marriages. A minister friend of mine said, "I have seen marriages that I thought were going to sink to the bottom of the sea revitalized when people began applying their faith to their marriages."

Points to Remember

- Faith is the foundation of the Christian live. Faith is a belief or pattern of beliefs. Faith is an essential ingredient in every successful endeavor including successful families.
- Hope is faith in action.
- Faith determines what we believe about marriages and families, how we see (perceive), who we are (character), and what we do (faith in expression).
- Faith is essential for preparing for marriage, for developing a successful marriage and family, for revitalizing troubled relationships, and for protecting the wellbeing of children in families.

Affirmations

- I am a kind, loving, and generous husband and father, and with God's help I am creating a wonderful family.
- I am thankful that God has given me a wonderful wife (or husband) and God is guiding us as we create a successful marriage.
- I am thankful that the Spirit of God is guiding me as I create a successful family.

Helpful Activities

What does it mean to have faith in your marriage and your family? How do you express your faith in your marriage and you family? Please answer the following questions.

What to you believe about marriage and family?

What do you believe about the spiritual purpose of your marriage and your family?

What do you believe about your ability to be a good husband or wife and to create a strong Christian marriage and family?

What do you do to help your family fulfill its highest mission and to help your family be strong and happy?

If you would like to do more, please write your goals for growth and how you can utilize your faith to achieve them.

CHAPTER 6

THE GREATEST OF THESE

> Beloved, let us love one another because love is from God; everyone who loves is born of God and knows God. Whoever does not love does not know God, for God is love.
>
> – I John 4:7-8

At 38 and 43, Karen and Jeff were a little older than the average newlyweds. Like most newlyweds, they got married because they thought they were in love. Also like most newlyweds, they got married hoping their love would last.

Karen and Jeff decided to try to keep their love alive by adopting a marital strategy based on competition. Usually, competition is not good for marriages, but this was different. Karen and Jeff decided they would compete to see who could serve the other more. They call it the "Do what you can do to out serve the other approach."

After almost ten years of marriage and two children, Karen says "It really works." Serving one another makes their lives joyful. "No matter what happens," she added, "it is difficult to get mad at someone who is doing his best to please you."

Karen and Jeff understand two of the most important secrets of marital success and their whole family benefits from it. The first is that a happy marriage is not about being served. We call this "getting our needs met." A good marriage is about serving. Marriage is first and foremost an opportunity to give. Karen and Jeff have discovered the paradox: the more we give the more joy we receive.

The other strength of Karen and Jeff's marriage is that the core of their marriage is also their faith. Karen says, "Every morning since we've been married, one of us says, 'This is the day the Lord has made' and the other says, 'Let us be joyful and be glad in it!' Our two boys say this too as part of the start to their day!"

What Is Love?

Love is one of the most important qualities of a successful marriage or strong family. But some types of love are suitable for marriage and some are not.

People often wonder, "What is love?" "How can I be sure I'm in love?" "How can we get our love to last?"

In the Heidelberg Disputation of 1518, Martin Luther said, "God's love does not find but creates, that which is lovable to it. Human love comes into being through that which is lovable to it" (Thesis #28). Christian character matters because it seeks to create love by being love even when people are not lovable.

The simplest way to know we love someone is that their wellbeing is at least as important to us as our own.

In *Mindful Loving: 10 Practices for Creating Deeper Connections,* Psychologist Henry Grayson says, "Love is the desire and willingness to give and to serve" (p. 206). In *The Road Less Traveled,* Psychiatrist M. Scott Peck describes love as "the will to extend one's self for the purpose of nurturing one's own or another's spiritual growth" (p. 81).When we love compassionately, our love affects our thoughts, feelings, intentions, and behavior.

Almost all positive aspects of family life, such as acting responsibly, accepting family members as they are, resolving conflict, and forgiving one another are based on commitment and compassion. The simplest way to know we love our family members is that their wellbeing is at least as important to us as our own. Loving is more important than being right, winning, getting our own way, or being served.

People who love compassionately can love as I Corinthians 13 teaches: love is patient, kind, not jealous or boastful, not arrogant or rude, does not insist on having its own way, rejoices in right, bears all things, hopes all things, believes all things, endures all things, and never ends. Without this kind of love nothing else matters.

Love is:	
Thoughts:	Respect, admiration,
Feelings:	Warmth and affection, closeness
Intention:	Determination to succeed, to act lovingly
Behaviors:	Acting lovingly, giving, caring, sharing
Outcomes:	Successful relationships, love returned.

You will know you have learned to live compassionately when your wife or husband is crabby and your only reaction is a desire to help.

Karen and Jeff seemed to understand that the kind of love that is suitable for marriage is based on commitment to the relationship and compassion for one another. When we love our partners compassionately we care deeply about their well-being. When they hurt, we hurt with them. We want to serve.

Passion may motivate us to develop close relationships but only compassion can keep us going through the struggles of the years.

Most couples do not compete to serve one another, but like Karen and Jeff, successful husbands and wives care about one another's wellbeing and they are willing to make sacrifices for one another and the relationship whenever needed. When they have conflicts, they respond compassionately by listening, trying to understand the problem, and by responding to their loved one's needs. When they have a conflict or problem, they will be concerned about how to solve it.

You shall love the Lord your God with all your heart, and with all your soul, and with all your mind. This is the greatest and first commandment. And the second is like it: You shall love your neighbor as yourself.   - Matthew 22:37-39

Love and Grace

"Love isn't love until it's unconditional."
                  - Marianne Williamson, *A Return to Love*, p. 40.

Compassionate love is based on thoughts and feelings of acceptance. Love does not evaluate things as right or wrong, good or bad (judging). Psychologist Carl Rogers used the term *unconditional positive regard* to describe the attitude of love that the *Bible* refers to as grace. In *Mr. Roger's Neighborhood*, Mr. Rogers told children, "I like you just the way you are." This is an attitude of grace, and it is the same attitude that leads to creating great marriages and strong families.

Accepting our loved ones sends a message that "I love you the way you are." Lack of acceptance weakens the foundation of the relationship because it sends a message of rejection. "I don't like you the way you are." "I expect you to be (or do) what I want."

It was easy to see that Robert was critical and controlling. Sharon could not get it right whether it was keeping financial records, dealing with her family of origin, or taking care of the children. Robert thought his way was better and their problems were the result of Sharon's shortcomings. She accepted his point of view, deferred to his power, and tried to please him. When he disagreed or challenged her, she would give in.

When Sharon and Robert were dating she was happy because she could be creative. She was delighted to be marrying someone who appreciated her and someone who listened to her. Someone who was not controlling and judgmental as her family had been. She was a natural leader and she felt free to take charge.

Robert enjoyed Sharon's gracefulness and enthusiasm and admired her independence. He was glad to be marrying someone who would be a strong partner and relieved to be free from his own family's expectation that he had to be the responsible one.

Robert and Sharon both believed they were a good team. They had similar attitudes, values, and goals. Both were intelligent, honest, and hard working.

But something happened along the way between the wedding and the current 15 years of marriage and two children. The attitude of grace that made their relationship so wonderful in the beginning had gotten lost under the responsibilities of marriage.

Sharon over-functioned as a rebel and under-functioned as a leader. Robert began over-functioning as family manager and under-functioning as a husband. He had stopped delighting in Sharon, appreciating her, and listening to her. His strong sense of responsibility and need for structure and predictability had overwhelmed the sense of freedom she had enjoyed so much.

The qualities that attracted Robert and Sharon to one another had been buried under years of frustration, disappointment, and anger; so had their hopes and dreams for a new life together.

As they reflected on the days of their courtship, Robert realized he missed Sharon's spunkiness and assertiveness. Sharon missed his acceptance and patience. They also realized that Sharon's gracefulness and ability to lead and Robert's ability to be accepting and supportive were still there. They could rediscover these qualities in one another and they began learning how to develop a renewed future based on mutual acceptance.

Extending ourselves for the wellbeing of the people we love means we are willing to change when circumstances require it. Robert and Sharon made a commitment to rediscover the attitude of grace that had been so meaningful in the beginning of their relationship.

The law of giving and receiving applies just as much to marriages as to any other aspect of life. Whether you give compassion or anger, you will receive as you give.

In the early years of our marriage Katie and I had a lot of conflict. And, we did not manage it well. We were both hurt and thinking we had failed again. In some ways it reminded me of my first marriage all over again. I kept trying to improve the relationship by getting Katie to change the behaviors that I thought were problems. But changing her was like trying to move a mountain.

I finally realized I was doing the four things John Gottman found that most couples who criticize one another, defend their own points of view, feel and express contempt when they are angry, and stonewall (withdraw emotionally) when they do not get their way get divorces. Couples who do not engage in these four behaviors do not get divorces.

has identified as predictors of divorce: criticism, defensiveness, contempt, and withdrawing. I had told myself I was just trying to improve the marriage by getting her to do things differently, defending myself from her criticism, and protecting myself emotionally. No matter what my excuses were, I was insisting my way was right and I was passively rejecting her when I got angry. I was destroying our relationship.

When I quit criticizing and began accepting Katie, the relationship began to improve. The most challenging parts for me were learning not to defend myself and not to withdraw when I felt criticized or disappointed. These were techniques I used to protect myself, I thought. I had to learn that when we had a problem, I needed to focus on what I could do to solve it and to replace defensiveness with curiosity by asking, "What would work better?"

I also had to learn that even though I was angry or not pleased about something, I could continue to be emotionally close and act lovingly. The displeasure or anger was temporary and based on a particular event. The problem had nothing to do with our love which was permanent. Understanding that having problems did not mean our love was flawed helped me to stay connected as I tried to resolve problems in loving ways.

I had to shift from an attitude of judgment to an attitude of grace. I also had to learn that my most important role in our marriage was to be the best husband I could be.

> TIP: You can improve your marriage by replacing criticism with acceptance, defensiveness with curiosity, contempt with compassion, and withdrawing with closeness.

To my surprise, Katie was suddenly different. My acceptance had allowed her to be the wonderful person I had fallen in love with and married. She also seemed to be more interested in me, my needs, and our relationship.

She changed, but she changed in her own way and in her own time. In *The Art of Loving,* Eric Fromm says "Love is based on the concern that the other person should grow and unfold as he or she is and for his or her own sake" (p. 28). Love leads to an attitude of grace (acceptance), because *love does not insist on having its own way* (I Corinthians 13).

Making small changes in our attitudes and behaviors can result in big changes in our marriages. We can solve even the most difficult marital problems when we are willing to become the solutions we need.

Unconditional love is not expressed exactly the same way toward our young children as it is expressed toward spouses. Children are future adults in training. As parents, we are in charge of shaping their lives and helping children learn appropriate behaviors.

Teaching is an expression of grace. Good-enough parenting starts with teaching. It helps children learn to be self-managing. The more appropriate behaviors children (and adults) know, the better equipped they will be for life and the more likely they will be to choose appropriate actions. Children need parents who teach them right from wrong, as well as the decision-making skills they need to succeed in life and relationships.

Even parents with the most well-mannered children need to set limits to keep children safe and help them learn to be capable and productive adults. Parents express love and respect—grace—toward their children when the limits they set are reasonable and for the children's own wellbeing, rather than because of a set of rigid parental attitudes and rules. Firm limits that are reasonable help children feel safe and loved.

Letting children take responsibility for their behavior and expecting them to do the things they are capable of doing for themselves are acts of grace. Defending children when they do something wrong teaches them that it is alright to behave inappropriately if they think they can get away with it.

Letting children learn from the consequences of their little stumbles can be an act of grace. Such experiences help them learn about causes and effects. What children learn from their little bumps and falls can help protect them from bigger mistakes later. If a toddler learns that running too fast may result in a fall and a bruised knee, he may understand as a teenager that driving too fast may result in a dangerous crash. Parents need to help their children learn from their mistakes, but always need to do their best to protect their children from serious harm.

In an atmosphere of unconditional positive regard, people—children and adults—can become all they can be. So can marriages and families.

Overcome Fear

> There is no fear in love, but perfect love casts out fear. For fear has to do with punishment, and he who fears is not perfected in love.   – I John 4:18 RSV

Every feeling and most behaviors are based on one of two primary emotions – love or fear. In his book, *Mindful Loving: 10 Practices for Creating Deeper Connections,* psychologist

Henry Grayson says that "All positive emotions such as joy, happiness, delight and affection, grow out of love. Negative emotions, such as anger, jealousy, guilt, envy, hurt, and rage, all grow out of fear."

Fear is the cause of almost all relationship problems. Loving another person makes us vulnerable. The more we love others, the more vulnerable we feel because the people we love can hurt us more than anyone else.

We do not usually think of ourselves as being afraid of our loved ones or our relationships. But fear masquerades in numerous guises: vulnerability, insecurity, hurt feelings, anger, and anxiety to name a few.

People have to take risks at every stage of relationships. What if I ask her for a date and she says "No?" "What if he doesn't love me as much as I love him?" "What if we get married and it doesn't work out?" "What if my child has a problem and I don't handle it?"

One of our most common fears is that family members do not love us. This fear is often expressed in statements like, "If she loved me she would (or wouldn't) . . . ." People who don't feel lovable are especially afraid their family members will not love them. Deep down, they may think (fear), "Perhaps I'm not good enough."

Realizing that our family members are separate from us is a source of insecurity. Some couples think that if they love one another, they will be the same in every way and that they will agree on everything. When they have a conflict they may think the people they expect to love them the most do not love them and are not on their sides.

TIP: Always remember, you and your spouse are on the same team.

Feeling hurt is a common mask for fear. When a wife says

something unkind, her husband may get his feelings hurt because he is afraid she does not respect him. When a husband looks at another woman with too much interest, his wife may feel hurt because she is afraid he does not think she is pretty enough. When a woman is not as attentive as her husband would like, he may get his feelings hurt because he fears she does not love him. People who experience fear as hurt feelings usually withdraw, which is a way of hiding from things that scare them.

Anger is another mask for fear. When a wife does not want to have sex, her husband may become angry because he is afraid she does not care about his needs. A wife whose husband disagrees with her may get angry because she is afraid he does not respect her opinions. When a wife disagrees with her husband, he may get angry because he is afraid she does not think he is smart enough. When a husband makes decisions without consulting his wife, she may get angry because his independence causes her to fear that she does not have enough power in the relationship. People who express fear as anger are prone to conflict, which is a way of protecting themselves by fighting.

Replace Fear-based Behaviors with Love-based Behaviors

There are two primary emotions: love and fear. There are three primary behaviors: approaching, avoiding, and attacking. When we love someone, we want to be closer. When we experience fear, we tend to avoid people (flee) or get into conflict (fight), or freeze.

We can transform our relationships by replacing behaviors based on fear with behaviors based on love. When we are tempted to behave unlovingly by being unkind, arrogant or rude, we can ask, "What am I afraid of?" "What might happen?" Many of our fears are based on fear of losing control, losing a loved one, or "losing face." When we understand our fears, we can overcome them and act lovingly.

Many fears are about events and circumstances that are not likely to happen. Once we realize a fear is unrealistic, we can let it go. Then, we can act lovingly instead of reacting to fear by getting angry or getting even.

> *Every human behavior is either an act of love*
> *or a plea for love.*

If the fear is real, we need to focus on solutions. When a man is afraid his wife may leave him, he needs to change the behaviors that are driving her away. She may become more loving when he does. When a woman is afraid she might be losing her husband, she needs to express more love by become closer instead of more distant, more accepting instead of rejecting. Even when relationships are in serious trouble, replacing fear with compassion can help us overcome the problems that are driving us apart.

A woman told her attorney that she wanted a divorce and she wanted to hurt her husband as much as she could. Knowing that this woman was arrogant and abrasive, the attorney suggested that her husband might not be hurt because she divorced him.

The attorney suggested that if she really wanted to hurt her husband she should go home and be the best and most loving wife she could be for a month. Cook her husband's favorite meals, make him comfortable at home, show respect and appreciation, and be kind and loving in every way. The attorney reasoned that after a month of loving care, her husband would know how much he had lost when his wife divorced him.

A month later the woman called the attorney to cancel the

appointment. She explained that she had fallen in love with her husband all over again.

At least one of these people, probably both, had been acting out of fear when their love relationship was deteriorating. Fear destroys people's willingness to give and serve, makes them rebellious, and angry – sometimes determined to get even. Fear drives people to do things that destroy loving relationships.

I do not know whether this story is true or where it came from, but I do know that it illustrates a profound truth about relationships: by giving love we create love in ourselves and in the people we love. One person changed and the marriage moved from competition to cooperation, from fear to love. We can all create miracles when we replace fear-based attitudes and behaviors with love-based attitudes and behaviors.

Fear-based behaviors are a cry for love, but reacting to fear almost always makes it less likely that relationships will be loving. Like the woman who wanted a divorce, our fears cause us to behave in ways that drive the people we love away from us. At first we may fight about our problems. If we are not able to settle them through conflict, we tend to withdraw emotionally. We may eventually decide we need to get a divorce which is an attempt to flee from the problems. Divorce is the ultimate act of fear for at least one of the partners.

When our family members act unlovingly, we can try to understand what is scaring them by asking, "What does he think might happen?" "What fear is driving her behavior?" Fear of being insulted? Of losing control? Of being unimportant? Of being abandoned? Of having to do things my way?

We can understand what our loved ones fear by listening carefully. What are our loved ones complaining about? People usually tell us what is bothering them, but sometimes in a subordinate clause or small phrase. Phrases such as "If you loved me (accepted me, respected me), you would (or wouldn't)," and "You don't care," are often the most important parts of people's sentences. They say, "I'm afraid you don't love me."

Men and women have some different fears about relationships. For women, the greatest fears are usually related to not being loved and safety. For men, it is fear of not being respected. Men desperately want to be respected by the women they love. When women complain about almost anything, men tend to hear criticism: "I am a disappointment to the woman I love." When women complain, men usually feel inadequate (fear). "She's upset with me because I'm a failure." Then men begin avoiding the women they love because they feel shame due to their perceived failures.

When our loved ones complain about something, we need to consider changing it. In relationships, who is right and who is wrong is seldom important. Changing how we deal with right-wrong conflicts shows that we care about our loved one's happiness and wellbeing more than we care about being right.

Mindy said she and her husband had been having a conflict about how to put the silverware in the dishwasher. She had shown Jerome how it should be done several times, but he kept doing it his way. Mindy felt hurt and angry because Jerome did not seem to care. One day she showed Jerome how she liked the silverware loaded and asked, "Would you do that for me?" Jerome seemed surprised, but after a brief pause said, "Sure, I'll do that for you." When she quit trying to be right and appealed to Jerome's compassion, Jerome was free to act lovingly.

In relationships, who is right and who is wrong is seldom important. Expressing love is what counts.

It is natural for us to want to defend ourselves when our loved ones are complaining or criticizing us. It is also natural to think that what we are doing is right because we have probably always done it that way.

People do not personalize problems like weeds growing in their gardens. No one would say, "I wanted to grow a garden, but the weeds wouldn't let me." We know that weeds are not "out to get us." But when "weeds" get in our relationships, we tend to take it personally as if our spouses are deliberately trying to make our lives difficult or put us down. We may go so far as to think, "I wanted to have a good relationship but she wouldn't cooperate."

Most conflicts are based on honest misunderstandings and personality differences. Such conflicts are as natural in families as weeds are in gardens. We need to give up fighting and put our efforts into managing the weeds.

Sebastian was interviewing for the position of minister in a new church. During the question and answer session, one of the members asked him what weakness he struggled with the most. Sebastian confessed that dealing with complaints and criticism was his biggest challenge. He admitted that he had a strong need to defend himself and he was often hurt by even the slightest complaint or criticism. He explained that he had once asked a friend for advice about how to deal with this problem. The friend told him that whenever someone complained or said anything critical about him, he should consider for at least an hour that the other person might be right and act accordingly. This was wise advice from a good friend and helper. Husbands and wives may find it is good advice too.

Whenever our spouses complain or criticize us, we should at least for an hour assume that they are right, and then act accordingly.

When our behavior is based on love, instead of defending

ourselves, we can be curious and ask, "What can I do to improve this?" "What would work better for you?" Changing the attitude of who is right and who is wrong can lead to simple changes that make a big difference in our relationships.

Conflicts are as natural in families as weeds are in gardens

How Does Love Cast Out Fear?

"A miracle is an authentic switch from fear to love"
- Marianne Williamson, *A Return to Love,* p. 163.

We are created in the image of God; therefore, we are the very essence of love. It is our nature to be kind, caring, and forgiving. The spiritual self naturally creates loving relationships.

As we grow up we form an image of who we are based on the values of our culture. We learn we are separate from others. From that time on there are two competing forces within us: ego, which is the worldly self and based on fear, and the spiritual self which is based on love.

Ego teaches us that winning is important, that we are what we have, that we are important when we are in control. Ego leads us to believe we need other people to do what we want them to do.

When our goal is to get our spouses to love us and serve us, we feel insecure because our wellbeing is based on the behavior of others. Even when we have loving relationships, we are insecure (afraid). "She may not love me as much as I love her," or "He may not do what I want him to do."

Ego is weak and fragile. When we become angry or hurt, ego may set off a cycle of negative interaction that may paralyze us emotionally, lead to emotional withdrawal (fleeing), or conflict (fighting). When these approaches do not work, people often think they need to flee further by getting a divorce.

We can form mature love relationships when our need to give love is greater than our need to receive love. When serving our loved ones is more important than being served as it was for Jeff and Karen, we do not have to worry about getting other people to do what we want them to do because our relationships are based on what we do rather than on what we want other family members to do. Our wellbeing depends on what we do. Serving others lets us focus on the process of being the best husbands, wives, parents, and children we can be.

TIP: Let serving your spouse be your only relationship goal for one month.

So what is the solution for managing the competition between the ego and the spiritual self? Consider the following proverb:

One evening an elder Cherokee told his grandson about a battle that goes on inside people. "My son," he said, "the battle is between the two 'wolves' inside us all. One is Evil. It is anger, envy, jealousy, sorrow, regret, greed, arrogance, self-pity, guilt, resentment, inferiority, lies, false pride, superiority, and ego. The other is Good. It is joy, peace, love, hope, serenity, humility, kindness, benevolence, empathy, generosity, truth, compassion, and faith."

The grandson thought about it for a minute and then asked his grandfather, "Which wolf wins?"

The old Cherokee simply replied, "The one you feed."

Developing a loving relationship based on Spirit is a

choice, a conscious decision. We decide to let the Spirit lead us instead of following the ego. Once we have made this decision, we can begin putting it into practice through our thoughts, feelings, intentions, and behaviors.

Edward Townley says, "When we surrender our own attempts to struggle and resist, and instead focus on allowing God to express through us, the stress and strain of life are instantly eased. Instead of wasting time and energy on resentment and anger, we gain the infinite strength and serenity of God" (p. 62).

When loving, giving, and serving others becomes more important to us than being loved, receiving, and being served, there is no need for fear, because perfect love will have overcome fear.

Try This Strategy

Prayer is a good technique for helping us overcome fear and create spiritual relationships. We can ask the spirit to guide us as we deal with the challenges of life and our relationships. I recommend having a small prayer rehearsed and ready for times of conflict which can erupt quickly. In the face of conflict, simply saying a simple prayer such as, "Holy Spirit, guide me now," can take away fear and help us respond lovingly. I prefer an affirmation such as, "The Spirit of God is guiding me as I solve this problem and create a loving family, and I am thankful." Or, "God is with me in this moment."

When we invite the spirit to lead us as we deal with a problem, psychologically we shift control from ego to Spirit.

Remember that if your behavior is not kind, it is based on ego. Only kind behaviors are based on leadership of the Spirit – no mater what others do.

Points to Remember

- Love is one of the most important qualities of a successful marriage or strong family. When we love compassionately, love affects our thoughts, feelings, intentions, and behaviors.
- Grace is a form of love based on acceptance. Love based on grace is unconditional.
- Children are adults in training. We express grace toward our children by teaching them appropriate behaviors, by setting reasonable limits, by letting children take responsibility for things they are capable of, and by letting children learn from the consequences of their behavior.
- Every feeling and most behaviors are based either on love or fear. Fear is the cause of almost all relationship problems.
- Fear in relationships masquerades in numerous guises such as vulnerability, insecurity, hurt feelings, anger, and anxiety. We can transform our relationships by replacing fear-based behaviors with love-based behaviors. Fear-based behaviors are a cry for love.
- Love can cast out fear. Fear is based on ego which is weak and fragile. When we express our love by serving, we do not need to win, have our way, or be served. When we let the Spirit overcome ego, we can overcome fear.

Affirmations

- God is helping me become a kind, loving, and generous husband and father or wife and mother.
- When my spouse is afraid, I respond with compassion.
- I always act lovingly no matter what other do.

Helpful Activities

Read I Corinthians 13 and discuss how can you apply the
characteristics of love it describes in your own marriage.

You may also use the scale below to rate the quality of the
love you bring to your relationship. Use 1 to indicate that the
quality does not describe your quality of love and 5 to indicate
it describes the quality of your love to a high degree.

Love is:

1 2 3 4 5	Patient
1 2 3 4 5	Kind
1 2 3 4 5	Not envious
1 2 3 4 5	Not boastful
1 2 3 4 5	Not arrogant
1 2 3 4 5	Not rude
1 2 3 4 5	Do not insist on my own way
1 2 3 4 5	Not irritable
1 2 3 4 5	Not resentful
1 2 3 4 5	Do not rejoice in wrongdoing
1 2 3 4 5	Rejoices in truth
1 2 3 4 5	Bears all things
1 2 3 4 5	Believes all things
1 2 3 4 5	Hopes all things
1 2 3 4 5	Endures all things
1 2 3 4 5	Never ends

Write a statement that described how well you are doing at
being a loving person based on the description in I Corinthians
13.

Are there any areas of your marriage or family that would be improved if you loved more like I Corinthians 13 teaches us to love?

How is your marriage and family affected by our lack of perfect love?

If you need to make improvements in any areas of your relationships, please develop a plan for growth and ask the Spirit to help you accomplish it.

Notes

Thank you to Karen Wright and Jeff Pribyl for the wonderful Karen and Jeff story and for permission for me to use it with their real names.

CHAPTER 7

IN THE IMAGE OF GOD

Then God said, "Let us make humankind in our image, according to our likeness. . . .
So, God created humankind in his image, in the image of God he created them; male
and female he created them.

Genesis 1:26-27

I did not understand the full meaning of the words, "in the image of God he created them," until I read a sermon by Dr. Fred Craddock who is one of the greatest Christian preachers of our times. He had a talent for helping people see things the way they had never seen them before.

In *The Cherry Log Sermons*, Dr. Craddock carefully described the creation including God's forming the human body and breathing the "breath of life" into it. Then God looked over the heavens and earth, and said, "It is good." God looked over all the creatures of the earth, and said, "It is good." God looked at the human, and said, "This one is just like me."

Dr. Craddock's words struck me like a lightening bolt. The idea that I was just like God was shocking. I had never let myself think that I was like God. It reeked with pride.

In *The I of the Storm,* Unity Minister Gary Simmons points out that it is difficult for us to think of ourselves as being like

God because we are not on the same level with Jesus. Simmons acknowledges that we are not on the same level as Jesus, but says, "You are on the same journey. You are in the process of awakening to God's idea of you. Jesus is your role model" (pp. 117-118).

We have the spirit of God within us, and we have godly qualities. We are able to love ourselves and others. We can accept people just the way they are, and we can forgive people who hurt us. We know the difference between right and wrong, and we can make appropriate choices. We are growing in Spirit and our goal is to become more like Christ. These qualities define who we are, our worth, and our abilities. We can develop the characteristics of God that are within us.

What about Pride?

The Bible clearly tells us that we are created in God's image; it must be true. But what about pride?

The psychological term for what the Bible refers to as "pride" is "narcissism." Narcissistic people act as if they think they are wonderful, have special gifts and powers, are entitled to special privileges, and know everything. They try to manipulate other people, and they will do almost anything for attention.

Narcissistic people act as if they are "full of themselves," because inside they feel empty. People with no self-esteem are so insecure that they believe they have to win to prove they are right. They are afraid to lose or be wrong. When people feel empty and worthless, they have to try to cover up their flaws with power, wealth, or a pretense of superiority. Their pride is the armor that protects them from feeling worthless, and the façade that they think makes them look important.

Narcissistic people feel a strong sense of shame. When people make mistakes it is natural to feel guilt. Feeling guilt lets us know we made a mistake and need to correct it. When people's self-esteem is very low, they tend to feel shame. People who feel shame think something is wrong with them and usually think it cannot be fixed. They hide their sense of shame behind a façade of importance. People with no self-esteem are afraid to be humble.

My being cold natured has helped me understand narcissistic people. My blood pressure runs a little low and my body does not seem to generate quite enough heat to keep me warm, especially during the long Minnesota winters. I am always looking for a seat near the fireplace or in a sunny window, an afghan to cover up with, or extra blankets for the bed.

It would only take a little more heat to keep me warm if I could generate it from the inside, but since I have to get it from outside sources such as blankets and heating pads, I have to get a lot of it and hope that enough of it will soak in to keep my body warm. I go to such great extremes to stay warm that I sometimes tell my wife, "This is ridiculous!"

Narcissistic people do not generate the basic feelings of comfort and security they need to enjoy life, and they are always trying to get the emotional resources they need for comfort, security, and happiness from external sources. It takes an endless supply of attention, complements, and support to keep them going. They go to great extremes because they are desperate.

Narcissistic people are filled with pride specifically because they do not know they are made in the image of God. They do not have a stable sense of identity and they are unable to love themselves. When they have problems that assault their big false egos, they are unable to soothe themselves emotionally enough to recover from the disappointments and problems of everyday life.

Because we know we are "just like God," Christians can be both confident and humble. We do not need to act powerful, pretend we are more intelligent than we are, or try to convince people we are wonderful in an attempt to cover up flaws. We know our worth.

Knowing we are created in the image of God can help strengthen us and our families by: (1) helping us develop healthy self-concepts, and (2) helping us develop self-esteem.

Self-Concept (Identity)

Self-concept is our perception of who we are. Some of the most important bases for our identity include gender (male or female), occupation (I'm a teacher, a plumber), sir name (the Brigmans are honorable people), and family roles (I'm the clown in the family, the one everyone talks to, or the outcast), or our values (I'm a person of integrity).

Our perception of our family of origin is one of the most influential shapers of our identities. My identity has been influenced by my paternal grandparents, whom I saw as intelligent, honest, decent, hardworking folk. I have their genes and I can see parts of Walter and Bess in myself.

My paternal grandparents were also my only model of a good marriage. In their own down-to-earth-country way Walter and Bess naturally did the things that lead to successful marriages. They were always friends and partners, were always kind to one another, always honored one another, and they always knew they were on the same team. They were humble country folk, but they knew how important they were.

Believing I came from honest, hard working, decent, intelligent people who valued their marriage and their family has helped me develop my own abilities as an individual and as a husband and father.

Since we are created in the divine image, we share characteristics of God just as we have characteristics of our parents and grandparents and just as our own children have some of our characteristics. We know that love, kindness, acceptance, and forgiveness are our nature.

When we know what we are made of, we know who we

are, how much we are worth, and what we can do.

Cheryl became interested in her family history after she had constructed a family tree as part of a treatment program. She was the daughter of an alcoholic father and codependent mother, and many of her family members had alcohol and drug problems, few had successful careers, and most were either divorced or had troubled families. Cheryl too had alcohol and drug problems, had been divorced, and had no career or direction in her life.

While she was working on her family tree, Cheryl had stumbled upon relatives who were high achievers. This discovery led her to begin to think that she was made of better stuff than she had realized. After all, she had some of the same genes those high-functioning relatives had. Cheryl made contact with some of these distant relatives and noticed that she even look like some of them.

Cheryl's new identity enabled her to develop a new vision for her life. She recovered from her alcohol and drug addictions, went to school and got a degree, got her first professional job, and decided to prepare for a successful marriage.

Moses grew up in the Egyptian royal family. As the son of Pharaoh's daughter, he was the prince of Egypt and consequently, the taskmaster of the Hebrew slaves. When he discovered that he was an adopted child, a Hebrew and the son of Yahweh, his identity changed and so did his life. He left the palace of Pharaoh, gave up his claim to the throne, and became the deliverer of his people, the Hebrew slaves.

When we identify with God, we will know who we are and what to do. We will naturally develop godly qualities because what we admire and desire is what we become.

In *The Great Stone Face* by Nathaniel Hawthorn, Ernest had spent his whole life admiring the great stone face in the mountain that towered above his small village. For many generations the people in the valley had believed that some day a great person who bore the image of the great stone face would come to their village and they would be blessed. The person in the great stone face was frequently described in terms of qualities such as kindness, compassion, wisdom, and generosity. Ernest spent his whole life admiring the great stone face, longing for this great person to come to the valley, and imagining what this great person would be like.

Over the years, Ernest came to be known in his village and throughout the valley for his wisdom and other virtues such as kindness and generosity. The great stone face had served as a teacher and model for his life, and Ernest became just like the person he had imagined in the face on the mountain. What he had thought in his heart. What he had hungered and thirsted for.

Self-Esteem

Self-esteem is the lens through which we see ourselves and others. It is true that we love our neighbors as we love ourselves.

Self-esteem is based on how much we value ourselves. It is based on our evaluation of attributes such as our personalities (I'm a nice person), abilities (I'm smart, a capable person), and physical characteristics (I'm attractive and desirable).

Being male or female is part of our identity. How we value our gender becomes part of our self-esteem. When a person is proud of his or her gender, it can be a source of self-appreciation. Understanding that both men and women are just like God and of great worth can help husbands and wives create strong relationships between equals who respect and honor one another.

Self-esteem is the lens through which we view ourselves

and the mold we use as we shape our lives and relationships. We become what we believe about ourselves and we usually create what we believe - the things we fear or the things we love. We tend to give ourselves what we think we deserve.

People with high self-esteem can make good mate selection decisions because they believe they deserve loving wives or husbands and because they believe that the women or men they are attracted to will be interested in them too. They will probably be able to become loving husbands and wives, fathers and mothers because they love themselves.

People who know they are made in the image of God can develop relationships with appropriate partners and make effective decisions about whether to get married. When they get married, they can accept their partners, solve problems, and forgive and reconcile when necessary. They have the courage to accept themselves and others as worthwhile even when they make mistakes.

When the spouse of someone with high self-esteem is grouchy, he will probably think it is because she had a frustrating day, or because she is tired. He may make excuses such as "everyone is grouchy sometimes." Since he loves himself and believes he is lovable, there is no reason for him to think his wife is grouchy because she does not love him even if she complains about something he did. He will probably assume that the problem is related to an issue or perhaps his wife is just in a "down" mood. Since he is not personalizing events, he can deal with the little issues that come up every day.

People with low self-esteem may have difficulty developing relationships with appropriate partners and making effective decisions. They may also have difficulty accepting their partners, solving problems, and forgiving and reconciling because they are afraid and they get hurt easily. Dealing with problems is difficult because they have to deal with perceived offenses and with their own feelings of inadequacy.

Since people with low self-esteem cannot love themselves,

they believe others do not love them either. When they have conflicts with their loved ones, they assume that their loved ones reject them too.

People with low self-esteem often believe, "I'm not smart enough," or "I'm not important enough." They may stay in relationships with people do not treat them kindly because they believe they do not deserve to be treated better.

> *Many marital problems – and most causes for not being able to solve them – are due to low self-esteem.*

People with low self-esteem project their beliefs about themselves on others. Then they blame others for the way they think other people see them. Here's how low self-esteem affected one couple. Notice how they made their fears come true.

- Deep down Jane did not believe she was lovable. (John did not believe he was lovable either).
- Consequently, she believed John did not love her. Since she did not believe he loved her, she noticed every little mistake he made as evidence that he did not love her. She discounted positive behaviors.
- She was hurt and angry at John for not loving her.
- Since she was afraid of being rejected, she had to protect herself by fighting (being big or strong, winning) or fleeing (keeping herself safe by withdrawing emotionally, physically, or both). People with low self-esteem tend to personalize ordinary events: "She gripes at me because she does not respect me" or "He treats me this way because he doesn't love me."
- When John responded from his fear by fighting or fleeing (we nearly always marry someone at our same level of emotional development), it confirmed Jane's belief that John did not love her because she believed that "If he loved me, he would not start a

fight (or reject me)." (Jane's fighting and fleeing also confirmed John's fear that Jane did not love him).

- Since Jane hated John for not loving her, she often lost her temper and acted unkindly. She did not have to be nice to him because he would probably reject her anyway. She could even reject him first. At least, she could punish him for not loving her and for wanting to reject her.

- There was no need for either of them to try to solve problems because neither one thought the other cared anyway.

- Jane and John were both miserable. They felt devastated, unloved, and rejected. Cheated. They had caused their fears to come true.

We all create our relationships and self-esteem is the basis by which we value ourselves and it influences our thoughts, feelings, intentions, and behaviors. Our behaviors usually create outcomes that confirm our original beliefs. Notice how my behavior can create positive or negative outcomes. Our behaviors usually create what we believe. We do not do this deliberately, but our perceptions of our experiences usually prove our beliefs are right – at least in our minds.

If I have high self-esteem, I will probably believe I am important and that people like me. If I step outside and see my neighbor in her yard, I will probably think she is glad to see me. So, I will smile and say, "Hello, Neighbor." She will probably notice that I am friendly (indicating that I like her) and she may respond, "Hello, Kelley. How are you today?" Her noticing me and being friendly will confirm my original belief that she likes me.

On the other, hand if I do not have high self-esteem, I will probably assume I am not very important and my neighbor probably does not like me. Instead of greeting her, I may wait for her to greet me if she is interested in being friendly with me. She will probably think that I am shy or that I do not want to be bothered. She may even think I did not say hello because I do not like her. When she does not say hello to me, it will confirm my original belief (fear) that she does not like me.

Parents with low self-esteem may think they have to make their children act just like a preconceived model of appropriate behavior. They may be afraid they will lose control, or their children will not turn out well. Or, they might be afraid they will be criticized or look like they are not doing a good job. Parents need to have the courage to be imperfect and still accept themselves. Successful parents need to have the courage to raise imperfect children too.

Realizing that we, our spouses, and our children are created in the image of God helps us treat ourselves and others kindly. When we know we are created in the image of God we can love ourselves and others as God loves us. Knowing we are created in the image of God contributes to high self-esteem. It helps us create strong families because we can be the best husbands and wives, mothers and fathers, and children we can be. It also helps us treat our husbands and wives and other loved ones with honor and respect because we know they are made in the image of God.

A Final Story

The messages of our culture teach us that we can only give what we have received. Therefore, people who came from families where they think they did not receive the love, nurture, and security they needed from their parents may see themselves as being disadvantaged for life.

We generally believe that defects from childhood become

emotional scars for life. People sometimes believe they can never overcome the hurts and disappointments of the past.

People who are angry and hostile often believe they are angry and hostile because their parents let them down, sometimes decades earlier. Once an alcoholic, always an alcoholic, we have been told. People with addictions and other problems often blame their early experiences with their parents for their current behaviors. Many people believe they cannot love themselves or others because they think they have never been loved.

In *Craddock Stories,* Mike Graves and Richard Ward relate a story told by my professor of preaching and a great storyteller, Dr. Fred Craddock. When he was in a distant city one Sunday morning Dr. Craddock walked to a little church near his hotel to attend worship.

The minister was tall and big, walked clumsily, almost falling as he lumbered down the aisle toward the pulpit. His head was misshapen and his hair askew. Thick glasses covered his clouded eyes. The Bible almost touched his nose as he read the Scripture. He pressured each word out of his mouth laboriously.

Professor Craddock, an internationally recognized authority on preaching, admitted that if he had read a copy of this minister's sermon he would have only given it a "C." It looked pretty ordinary. But the love he expressed to his flock and the love they expressed in return were extraordinary.

Dr. Craddock lost consciousness of the man's appearance and mannerisms when he started reading from I Corinthians 13, "love is patient; love is kind; love is not envious or boastful. . . . How could this grotesque creature be so full of love?" I didn't understand," he said. "I started remembering things that I shouldn't have remembered – all those stories about people who have grotesque features sometimes are granted a special quality of affection. *Beauty and the Beast* or Victor Hugo's *Hunchback of Notre Dame*, so ugly and yet so beautiful in his love and capacity for affection" (p. 50).

Dr. Craddock wanted to get to know this remarkable preacher, so he waited after the service to meet him. As people were shaking hands with the minister, Dr. Craddock heard a woman tell him she wished she could know his mother (Craddock assumed she did not understand how this man could be so filled with love either). He told her, "My mother's name is Grace."

As they chatted, Dr. Craddock asked the minister about his unusual response to the woman who wished she could know his mother: "My mother's name is Grace" (p. 50).

"When I was born," he said, "I was put up for adoption at the Department of Family Services. But as you can see, nobody wanted to adopt me. So I went from foster home to foster home, and when I was about sixteen or seventeen, I saw some young people going into a church. I wanted to be with young people, so I went in, and there I met grace – the grace of God."

Conclusion

The answer to this minister's ability to give so much love when he had come from such an insecure childhood is simple but profound. Christianity holds that we can be transformed. We can overcome deficits from childhood. We can replace ineffective interpersonal skills with effective skills. We can overcome addictions. We can love ourselves and others regardless of past experiences.

This minister's identity and his life were changed when he learned he was "just like God." He was no longer a grotesque person, unloved and rejected. He was a child of God. He could express the character of God by loving himself and by treating other people as God would treat them. Because he expressed the love of God, he inspired love from others.

When we know that grace is our mother, we too can treat others with loving kindness, and we can receive loving kindness in return.

I am no longer shocked when I think about being "like God." I am thankful that can see parts of God in myself just I can see parts of my grandparents in myself and parts of myself in my own children.

Just as I am expressing characteristics of my paternal grandparents when I am honest, hard working, and decent, I am expressing the characteristics of God when I live by faith, when I love myself and others, when I forgive people who have hurt me. I am expressing the characteristics of God when I believe in families and when I believe that that I can create a successful family.

Points to Remember

- Knowing we are created in the image of God helps us create happy marriages and strong families because it helps us develop healthy self-concepts and high self-esteem.
- Self-concept is our perception of who we are and what we are worth. Because we have characteristics of God our essence is love, kindness, acceptance, and forgiveness are our nature.
- Our Self-esteem is the lens through which we view ourselves and the mold we use to shape our lives and relationships. We usually create what we believe we deserve. People with high self-esteem can create happy marriages and strong families because they know how much they are worth.

Affirmations

- I am a child of God. I am love, patience, kindness,

forgiveness, and grace.
- I am a child of God, made in God's image, and I am thankful.
- I treat my wife/husband with honor and respect because she/he is made in the image of God.

Helpful Activities

Who Am I Exercise

Who are you? Describe yourself physically, mentally, psychologically, and spiritually.

Deep in your heart, who do you believe you are and what do you believe about your own worth?

If you really were "just like God," what would you do?

Do it.

Self-Esteem Checklist

Please answer the following questions about characteristics of self-esteem. People with high self-esteem would probably answer all of these questions with a SA (Strongly Agree) or A (Agree). Any answers of U (Undecided), D (Disagree), or SD (Strongly Disagree) would indicate areas that need growth.

SA A U D SD   I am happy.

SA A U D SD   I like myself the way I am.
SA A U D SD   I would not want to be anyone else.
SA A U D SD   I deserve to be loved and respected.
SA A U D SD   I love and respect myself.
SA A U D SD   I feel that the most important people in my
               life respect me.
SA A U D SD   I am a good person.
SA A U D SD   I believe I can do the things I need to do.
SA A U D SD   I can forgive myself when I make mistakes.
SA A U D SD   I do not need other people to tell me when
               I've done a good job.
SA A U D SD   I do not need the approval of other people
               to feel good about myself.
SA A U D SD   I do not worry about what other people
               think of me.
SA A U D SD   I can admit it when I make mistakes.
SA A U D SD   When I make mistakes, I still feel like I am
               a good person.
SA A U D SD   I am comfortable being myself.
SA A U D SD   I enjoy other people.
SA A U D SD   I always treat other people with kindness
               and respect, even those who disagree
               with me.

Scores of U, D, or SD would indicate areas that need growth. Perhaps you could read the biblical account of creation in Genesis and think about what it means to be made in the image of God. Develop a plan for spiritual growth.

CHAPTER 8

SEVENTY TIMES SEVEN

The main function of love is to forgive.
- Henry Grayson, *Mindful Loving: 10 Practices for Creating Deeper Connections*, p. 203.

At no time are we more like God than when we forgive.

One Monday in October 2006, a local milk truck driver entered an Amish elementary school in Nickel Mines, Pennsylvania. He dismissed everyone except ten girls. Moments later the troubled man shot the girls, killing five and severely wounding the others. Then, he killed himself.

Within hours members of the Amish community, including at least one father of a girl who was slain, visited the killer's widow. They told her they had forgiven her husband and that they would not hold his crime against her or her family. They offered her and her family their support during their time of grief.

News of the shooting traveled quickly. It was shocking. But the response of the Amish people toward the killer and his grieving family stunned the world.

Some people praised the Amish parents for their compassion. Others believed that forgiving anyone who had committed such a horrible crime was psychologically unhealthy or a denial of the innate human need for justice.

Most people could not understand how anyone could forgive someone who had hurt them so much.

Fortunately, most of us never experience a trauma as painful as having our children murdered. But all of us deal with unpleasant situations that require forgiveness. People in the community or workplace who tell lies about us. Friends who betray us. People who steal from us or cheat us.

The people who can hurt us the most are the ones we love the most, the people in our families. Some families have to deal with big issues such as infidelity or domestic abuse. All families have to deal with ordinary issues that require forgiveness - husbands and wives who are forgetful or short-tempered, parents who are impatient, children who are demanding or uncooperative, and loved ones who compete unfairly for family resources.

For most of us forgiveness is the work of a lifetime. Who among us has forgiven everyone who has ever hurt him? Holds no grudges? Never keeps score? Never feels entitled to get even?

Who among us does not wonder if someone has forgiven her? Or, has forgiven herself completely?

This chapter has been difficult to write because I have had to deal with my own forgiveness issues: people I may not have completely forgiven, mistakes I have made, and people who may not have forgiven me.

This chapter may also be difficult to read because it challenges all of us to deal with our forgiveness issues. Forgiveness and reconciliation are two of our biggest challenges; they are also two of our most important opportunities.

Newborn butterflies have to work hard to get out of their cocoons, but the struggle helps them develop the strength they need to fly when they do get out. Without this struggle, the butterflies will die. Without forgiveness and reconciliation, all our families would die.

Forgiveness is especially important since most family members have to deal with the same kinds of problems over and over. Many of the problems family members have to deal with are related to personality characteristics that are not likely to change. My ambivalence and lack of organization show up over and over in any area of life no matter how hard I try. Sometimes I talk too much without noticing until it is too late. Even though I try, my wife will probably always have to tolerate some lack of organization, some ambivalence, and my occasionally talking too much. She will probably need to forgive me for these irritations over and over. If my behavior exceeds what she is able to accept and forgive, we will have problems.

Forgiveness and Reconciliation

Forgiveness is pardoning someone whom we believe has offended us or harmed us. Forgiveness is a decision based on a thought. The Amish parents forgave the killer when they made a decision to give up their "right" to get even, to be angry, to hold a grudge, or to punish.

Reconciliation is the process of restoring the emotional closeness that was reduced or destroyed when someone hurt or offended us. When family members reconcile they can become close again.

The relationship between forgiveness and reconciliation may help us understand why forgiveness is always the right thing to do, and why it is both spiritually and psychologically healthy. It will also help us understand when reconciliation is appropriate.

When the Amish parents of the slain girls forgave the killer, they chose not to hold on to feelings of anger, not to hate, and not to get even.

But if the killer had lived, it would not have been appropriate for the Amish people to allow him to go back to the school or to remain in the community. Even after forgiving the killer, it would have been appropriate for the Amish parents to have cooperated with law enforcement to apprehend him and with the court system to convict him.

If the Amish parents had been friends with the killer before the offense, it would not have been appropriate for them to continue the friendship after the killings even though they had forgiven him. Their forgiveness did not cancel the moral responsibility of the Amish people to keep themselves, their families, and their community safe.

Likewise, forgiving people who have hurt us or offended us does not mean that we should automatically accept them back into our lives or make ourselves vulnerable to them again.

To reconcile, people usually need to be confident that they can establish a relationship that will not repeat the problems of the past. It may not be appropriate:

- To reconcile with people who are dangerous or who may harm us again.
- To reconcile with people who have treated us unkindly and have shown no evidence that we can have a respectful relationship with them in the future.
- To continue living with an abuser and subjecting our children to life in a dangerous environment.
- To reconcile with people who continue to treat us unkindly.

When we reconcile we restore the relationship to what it was before the offense, or establish a new relationship that promises to work better than the old one. When we forgive, but choose not to reconcile, we can leave the old feelings of anger and resentment behind and make a new beginning without the old relationship.

Benefits of Forgiveness and Reconciliation

Tip: You cannot feel love and resentment at the same time. Therefore, you cannot love as long as you hold resentments.

Jesus teaches us that we need to forgive and we need to be forgiven. Both of these needs are acknowledged in the Lord's Prayer – "Forgive us our debts (trespasses) as we forgive our debtors (those who trespass against us)."

No one can love himself or others or have close relationships with other people without forgiving himself and others, and without having the forgiveness of friends, loved ones, even strangers.

We can forgive our former spouses, and for our children's sake we should, even though reconciliation is not likely. Forgiving our former spouses ends the bitterness and allows everyone involved including their children to have a new life.

Forgiveness is beneficial to the people who are forgiven. If the killer of the Amish children had lived, this troubled man could have known that even though he had done something awful, the people whom he had harmed had been compassionate enough not to hold the offense against him. Knowing he had been forgiven could have helped lift his burden of anger, guilt, and shame. Being forgiven might have helped him find a renewed sense of his own worth. It might have helped him forgive himself and others.

Mike Carlucci's life was transformed by three simple words: "I forgive you." These words were from the father of

Scott Everett whom he had killed. When Mike received those words he said he got down on his knees and prayed for forgiveness and he believed he had received it. He felt a sense of release from the burden.

Forgiveness is beneficial to the people who forgive. After Walter Everett's son, Scott, was killed, he said his rage and depression were tearing his life apart. He prayed asking God how he could overcome his anger. When Mike Carlucci told the court, "I'm sorry I killed Scott," Everett believed that God had shown him how to overcome his anger. A few weeks later he wrote to Carlucci prison and told him, "I forgive you." Walter Everett acknowledged that his life would never be the same as a result of having his son killed, but forgiving Carlucci did let him begin the long process toward recovery. Forgiving is the only way we can overcome feelings of anger, resentment, hate, and the desire to get even.

In the case of the Amish parents forgiveness was a gift to themselves: the gift of not holding on to the hate and resentment and not passing it down to their other children. Forgiving also allowed the parents to grieve their loss without needing to get revenge.

The greatness of the loss and the depth of the pain of the Amish parents made forgiving the killer even more necessary. How could they ever go on with life as long as they felt such pain? They would never be the same, by forgiving they could begin to heal and they could use their energy learning how to go on with their lives.

As in the case of the Amish parents, forgiveness does not always come easily or quickly, but through forgiveness people can eventually heal the pain in their hearts, feel better, find peace, and have closer relationships with the people they love. Forgiveness can even help people heal war-torn relationships.

We have control over our ability to forgive, so, we can set ourselves free from hate and anger no matter what others choose to do. We can also heal our relationships with our friends, neighbors, and loved ones.

"When you find peace within yourself, you become the kind of person who can be at peace with others. – Peace Pilgrim

Reconciliation allows people to become close again. This is especially important for families. It may be okay to be a little distant from some family members. Most of us also have an Uncle Bill that we really do not like, cousins we have never really known, or family members we do not trust. But to have happy marriages and strong families it is necessary to stay emotionally connected to our closest family members – husbands, wives, parents, children, and most members of our extended families.

Small acts of reconciliation are fairly easy and they are a natural part of everyday life in most families. One of my students described reconciliation in her family: "We always shared love together. Even after conflict, we gave each other a hug or kiss and life went on." Reconciliations following serious family problems or prolonged periods of conflict can be intense. But they are usually worth the struggle because they can restore relationships with people whom we love.

We must develop and maintain the capacity to forgive. He who is devoid of the power to forgive is devoid of the power to love. There is some good in the worst of us and some evil in the best of us. When we discover this, we are less prone to hate our enemies.   - Martin Luther King, Jr.

As long as you feel the grudge, you have not forgiven.

When We Need Forgiveness

When we make mistakes and offend others, we need to take responsibility for our behavior. An apology is usually suitable for little discourtesies like being late to dinner, talking too much or being a little grouchy. Asking for forgiveness is usually more effective than an apology for dealing with serious problems such as overspending the checking account, embarrassing our spouses in public, or having a flirtation or affair.

Asking for forgiveness often works better than an apology because it is stronger. It also implies contrition and a willingness to make amends for past offense s and to correct the problem. When we ask for forgiveness, the other person participates by agreeing to forgive, or refusing to forgive. When both people are involved, forgiveness becomes a mutual process.

For many people, forgiving themselves is the hardest forgiveness issue they ever struggle with. Many people who have difficulty forgiving themselves do not feel worthy of forgiveness. They are not only unable to forgive themselves, but they are also unable to accept forgiveness from God or others because they feel a deep sense of shame.

Feelings of guilt let us know we have done something inappropriate and can motivate us to correct the mistake. When we feel shame, we treat ourselves as if something is wrong with us. We may think we are not worthy of forgiveness.

To forgive ourselves and others, we need to understand that we deserve forgiveness. Having made a mistake or many mistakes does not make us any less a child of God or any less worthy of forgiveness. Realizing that we are created in the divine image and that we are the objects of God's love and forgiveness, can help us understand how truly important we are and how truly good we are. The following suggestions can help us forgive ourselves and others.

- Realize that both you and the person who has hurt you are both good people, each made in the image of God.
- Realize that seldom is a problem caused by only one person; accept responsibility for your part of the problem.
- Study biblical passages about forgiveness. Pray and meditate on forgiveness and affirm that you are a good forgiver.
- Realize that people who offend us are usually responding to their own fears rather than having malevolent motives.

When We Need to Forgive

When we have been offended, we can choose to forgive and let go. Most successful people are careful about letting themselves feel offended because when they take offense they have to carry the burden of feeling offended.

When we do need to forgive, it is usually easier to forgive when we can discuss problems, especially if the offending person apologizes.

Sometimes people wait for the offending person to apologize or ask to be forgiven. But, the offending person may understand the issue differently, may not be aware that he or she did something hurtful or offensive, or may be afraid to admit fault.

It is not always possible to discuss the problem with the offender or to work out a solution. The person may be unwilling or too angry to have a productive discussion, or even dead. Forgiveness is all the more necessary when problems cannot be fixed. When we forgive, we can heal even if the other person does not apologize, or if the problem does not get solved.

The Process of Forgiving

The need for forgiveness begins with an event or a pile up of events that someone perceives as offending or causing harm. Sometimes we make mistakes that offend or harm others; sometimes others hurt or offended us. We need to learn to forgive others and ourselves, and to accept forgiveness.

Forgiveness is an act, but like so many seemingly simple acts, it is a process—often a long and demanding process. The process of forgiving is complex and includes:

Thoughts: Make a decision to forgive.
Feelings: Give up feelings of anger and resentment.
Intentions: Give up intentions to get even or to get revenge; replace with intention to forgive.
Behaviors: Do not retaliate with unkind words or behaviors.

The following steps can help us work through the process of forgiving. People who have serious issues, may need to allow extra time to work on this process. Some steps will probably be more difficult than others. Some steps may need to be done over and over.

Forgiveness is rarely easy, except for God, but in the end, the benefits are well worth the effort for everyone involved.

Begin with Prayer, Meditation, and Affirmations

Whenever we deal with conflict or other relationship challenges, we need to begin by seeking the leadership of Spirit. Prayer and meditation are good ways to let the Spirit lead us. After a few minutes of meditation people often understand problems more clearly and may even understand what they need to do to solve them. We can also pray for the faith and courage we need to ask for forgiveness when we hurt others and for the faith and courage we need to forgive others who have hurt us.

Affirmations such as "The Spirit of God is guiding me as I forgive _____," can help us open our hearts to the leadership of the Spirit. Affirmations such as "I can do all things through him who gives me strength," (Phil. 4:13) help us to be assured that with God's help we can forgive even the most hurtful offenses.

It is important to pray for the persons we need to forgive, especially if we are having difficulty forgiving; we also need to pray for our ability to forgive.

Analyze the Event or Events

Once a harmful or offensive event has occurred, we need to develop a clear and tangible definition of the problem. We need to stick with the facts and define the problem in terms of the behaviors that are bothering us rather than on our perceptions of the offender's personality or motives. It is important to stay focused on the small problems that started the disagreement rather than on the hurt feelings that were caused by the way we fought about it.

Whenever we experience a conflict or hurtful event, we need to begin by asking:

"Is my perception of the event accurate?"
"How could I see this differently?"
"How would the other person describe the event?"
"How did I contribute to the problem?"

Once we understand the problem, we need to determine whether we have been harmed or offended. We can ask, "How have I been tangibly affected?" Be specific. Did the offense result in harm to your body or property? Did it cost money? Or, only hurt feelings?

If no tangible damage has been done, or if the problem falls within the range of behaviors that you can accept, you can simply let go. If you decide you have been harmed and the problem requires forgiveness, you can ask yourself,

"What is the best way to deal with this problem?"

"What do I need to do to be able to forgive?"

Look for Positive Qualities

> We must develop and maintain the capacity to forgive. He who is devoid of the power to forgive is devoid of the power to love. There is some good in the worst of us and some evil in the best of us. When we discover this, we are less prone to hate our enemies.   - Martin Luther King, Jr.

When we have been hurt or offended, it is natural for us to become extremely aware of our pain and to concentrate on the faults of the offender. Thinking almost exclusively about another person's faults demonizes that person and makes forgiveness almost impossible.

None of us is perfect and none of our enemies is all bad. However, focusing only on their faults makes them appear so.

When we need to forgive, we need to give extra attention to recognizing the positive qualities of the persons whom we think have hurt or offended us. We can also give some attention to thinking about our part in the problem. Problems in relationships are never the result of the misbehavior of one person.

Recognizing the positive qualities of the person who has hurt us, and recognizing how we played a part in the problem or at least how we are responsible for how we understand the problem can help us put the problem in perspective. Understanding can also help us forgive ourselves and others.

Get in Touch With What You Believe

> "Real power is acting in our own best interests, and your long-term emotional best interests depend entirely on acting according to your deepest values"
> - Steven Stosny, *Love Without Hurt,* p. 160.

People who are most successful in life and relationships base their decisions and behavior on their own core values. If they believe love is important, they behave lovingly. If they believe forgiveness is important, they forgive. No matter what others do.

The Amish parents whose children were slain were able to forgive because they were Christians. Even when they were experiencing deep anguish, they took responsibility for living according to their values—no matter what others did. Their forgiveness of the killer of their children was based on a decision to do what they believed was right. It had nothing to do with the killer, what he did, or their feelings. They were following Jesus' words, "Forgive us our debts as we forgive our debtors."

When we need to forgive, we need to focus on who we are and what we believe about forgiveness instead of focusing on what others did or how we might feel.

As Christians, we forgive because we are followers of Jesus' teachings and because we know forgiveness is important. We can get in touch with our own values about forgiveness by asking,

"Do I believe I should forgive all offenses?"

"Is forgiveness always healthy?"

"Do my beliefs about forgiveness help me to be happy and healthy?"

"Will forgiving help me have good relationships with the
people I love?"

Focus on Your Goals

Nelson Mandela grew up in the racially divided Union of
South Africa. Even as a young adult he opposed the injustices
and oppression of racism through his leadership in the African
National Congress which challenged the white-ruled government for the rights of non-white people. Sometimes violently.

As a result, Mr. Mandela was accused of crimes against
his country and sentenced to life in prison. He had spent
almost 30 years when he was freed largely due to world-wide
political pressure to release him and to end apartheid. Once
released, he resumed his leadership in the African National
Congress and eventually helped establish a multi-racial
democracy in the Union of South Africa for which he and then
president DeKlerk were awarded the Nobel Peace Prize. Then,
in 1994, Mr. Mandela was elected President of the Union of
South Africa in the first multi-racial election in his country.

It would seem reasonable to expect that Mr. Mandela
would be bitter about the way Blacks had been treated and
about his own imprisonment. It would also be reasonable to
expect that as president, he would take advantage of the
opportunity to favor his own race and probably to get even
with people who had supported the oppressive white
government for so long.

But reconciliation was Mr. Mandela's goal.

When we know what is most important to us, we know
where to devote our time and energy. No matter what people
did to him, Nelson Mandela lived according to his own goal
for reconciliation for South Africa. He did not react to
problems of the past or the criticism of his opponents. No
matter what others did, he refused to hate, to hold resentments,
or to get even.

Mr. Mandela said, "This is no time to celebrate petty revenge; it is time to build our nation." He said, "The rainbow nation starts here. Reconciliation starts here. Forgiveness starts here too." He said, "If there are dreams about a beautiful South Africa, there are also roads that lead to their goal. Two of these roads could be named Goodness and Forgiveness."

We should be aware that if we have dreams about beautiful relationships with the people we love, goodness and forgiveness are the roads that will take us there. If our goal is to have close and loving relationships, then we need to learn to be good forgivers and forgive.

> *"Forgiveness liberates the soul; it removes fear."*
> - Nelson Mandela

Develop a Healing Strategy

Forgiveness and compassion can change a troubled past into a happy present.

A healing strategy is a way of looking at events that can help us overcome the painful effects of the problem. We can look at our beautiful new car all smashed up and say, "I'm just thankful no one was killed." Or "It could have been so much worse." Such a perspective helps us overcome the pain of having the new car wrecked by comparing what happened to what could have happened.

My cousin, Norah, and I both came from families where we were neglected and abused, she more than I. For many years I blamed my parents. They were hardly more than children themselves when they divorced, but I always felt abandoned and held resentments that hurt me and the people I loved.

Norah was more compassionate. She told me that our

parents were never able to overcome their demons. She understood that their lives were filled with problems they never learned how to manage. She also said that she is thankful that we have been able to overcome our demons. She focused on how we turned out rather than on how hard we had to struggle to get where we are. She thought we were lucky. She says, "We were blessed."

Norah's perception changed the way I looked at my own experiences. The past did not change, nor did my parents, but my anger and resentment changed to compassion and forgiveness. I changed.

Trying to see problems from an optimistic and productive perspective can help us solve them. The way we think about problems can help us get in the right frame of mind to forgive and heal.

- Believing his wife did not mean to hurt him can help a husband believe that her motives were good even though she made a mistake. "She's got a good heart; she just has trouble controlling her temper."

- Believing he did not understand can help a wife believe that her husband did not know that what he was doing would hurt her, or he did not know any other way to behave. "He just didn't know what else to do."

- Believing he is sorry for what he did lets a wife believe that even though he may have hurt her, he feels remorse for the mistake. "I know he's sorry he hurt me; he just can't say it."

- Believing that there is a purpose for everything lets people believe that something beneficial will come as a result of the problem. "I know there's a purpose for this problem."

-

The following suggestions may help us develop a positive frame of mind for problem-solving, forgiving, and healing.

- Look at your spouse and try to see the image of God in her or him.
- Be aware that any mistakes your spouse has made were probably based on fear, lack of understanding, or lack of relationship skills.
- Put yourself in the same place as the person who hurt you. Try to understand the other person's point of view.
- Focus on positive memories about the offending person.
- Remember times when you have made mistakes.
- Make excuses for your family members; and, hold yourself responsible.
- Remember, relationships are endless cycles of events, actions and reactions. No relationship problem is caused by only one person or one event. Focus on your own part in the problem and take responsibility.
- Remember forgiveness is beneficial to you. It is the only way you can heal the pain in your heart and the only way you can be psychologically and spiritually healthy.

Overcome Fear

I have worked with couples who were locked in pain and fear, unable to let go and feel their love. I would usually make a statement such as, "I don't who is going to reach out to solve this problem first" (implying that I believed both were going to do it, I just did not know who would do it first). Then I would say, "Usually the one who feels stronger is the one reaches out first" (changing the act of reaching out first to a show of strength instead of an admission of weakness).

Fear is one of the biggest roadblocks to forgiveness. Sometimes people fear that if they forgive they are being weak and losing power. "If I forgive her, she will walk all over me—even more." They also fear that others may think they are weak. "If I forgive him, people will think I am weak and they will not respect me."

It takes strength and courage to be good forgivers. Forgiveness is not a function of ego because ego is too weak to forgive; forgiveness is a function of the Spirit because it requires strength and courage.

Some people think forgiving means forgetting that an offense ever occurred. But forgiving always acknowledges that the offense did occur. Others are afraid that if they forgive they may be victimized again. People often fear that it is unfair for them to be treated unkindly and then have to forgive the people who have offended them. Such attitudes can keep people locked in pain and resentment.

In *The Secret According to Jesus: Living a Joyful Life,* Unity minister Edward Townley says, "Noting is more damaging to our strength and wellbeing than allowing stress and anger to block us from feeling the power and joy of God's love. We never have to allow anyone or anything to create that block; by allowing God's eternal Presence to express, we will always prevail" (p. 62).

We can learn to identify the fears that make forgiving difficult by asking:

"What am I afraid of?"
"What will happen if I forgive her?"
"How will I feel if I forgive him?"
"What do I have to lose?"
"What will people think about me if I forgive her again?"

Anger and hate are the armor that protects the fearful.

When we understand what is causing us to be afraid, we can determine whether our fears are realistic. If they are not likely to happen, we can let them go. If the fear is real we can still forgive, but we may need to protect ourselves by not putting ourselves in situations where we are vulnerable again.

When we can overcome our fears, we can usually see that the people we have feared are being blocked by their own fears. When we respond to their fears instead of getting angry and holding grudges, we can sometimes help them overcome the fear so they can respond more lovingly too.

Overcome Cultural Influences

When the Amish parents forgave the killer, they were doing what they had been "cultured" to do all their lives. They had been prepared to be good forgivers long before the tragedy occurred.

Religion is at the heart of every aspect of Amish life. The Amish people believe and practice the teachings of the Bible about forgiveness literally. They read the Bible daily and recite the words, "Forgive us our debts as we forgive our debtors" from the Lord's Prayer several times each day. Through their prayers they had practiced forgiveness over and over.

When a culture values forgiveness, forgiving becomes rewarding. For instance, people receive internal rewards—feel good about themselves—as a result of believing they have done the right thing. When people believe they are forgiven as they forgive, they also feel rewarded because they were forgiven because they forgave.

The Amish people also live among a community of friends and family who value forgiveness and encourage one another to forgive. The Amish culture also supports forgiveness and honors people who forgive people who have harmed them. Many of the folk stories they tell in their families (instead of watching television) are about people who forgave their killers before they were executed. The strong community support the

Amish people have helps them live their faith even when it is difficult. When the people who are important to them respect and honor them for forgiving they are again rewarded.

Most of us believe the words from the Lord's Prayer, "Forgive us our debts (or trespasses) as we forgive our debtors (or those who trespass against us)" clearly mean that we should forgive others. But many of the attitudes of our culture are not compatible with Christian values.

Jesus taught us to forgive. But, our society tends to follow a philosophy which is based on human reason as its source of truth and that values qualities such as fairness, equality, justice, and basic concepts of right and wrong. Such a philosophy works well for a diverse society that respects the rights of all people to make their own choices and live their own lifestyles. But it falls far short of spiritual values such as compassion, grace, and forgiveness that are so vital for close relationships. One of the reasons forgiveness seems so illogical and is so difficult for us to do is that we live in a society that believes in fairness and justice, but forgiveness requires compassion and mercy.

> "Whenever we violate our deepest values, we automatically experience guilt, shame, and anxiety"
> – Steven Stosny, *Love Without Hurt,* pp. 161-162).

It is more difficult to learn to be good forgivers in a society that values fairness and justice more than compassion and mercy and values personal freedom and growth more than close relationships. We all have to make decisions about what is important and what we believe and to find the courage to live according to our own faith and values.

Make a Decision and Take Action

Forgiving takes place when we make the decision (a thought) to forgive. The Amish parents forgave when they made a decision to give up their anger, not to hate the killer, and not to get revenge. Their forgiveness was a decision to get over the problem rather than letting anger and resentment control their lives.

After forgiving the Amish parents still had to struggle with the pain and grief related to the death of their children, but forgiving was a commitment to deal with the feelings of pain without hating or trying to get even. They focused on their commitment to forgiveness as they dealt with their grief. Forgiving did not resolve their pain and grief immediately but forgiving allowed them to deal with their grief without the hate or anger.

The Amish people at Nickel Mines could spend the rest of their lives hating the killer. The more they hated him the more they would become like him.

Follow Through

A decision to forgive needs to be followed with action, sometimes over and over. It requires a decision to keep trying. Sometimes people are able to forgive and go on with their lives and families. Some hurts are so deep that it can take time to overcome feelings of grief associated with the loss.

One minister compared forgiveness to ringing a church bell. When we forgive we let go of the rope, but it still takes time for the bell to stop ringing. And when we forgive, we let go of the bitterness, but it takes time for the pain to go away.

It is difficult to imagine that the Amish parents did not have to keep forgiving the killer over and over – perhaps every day. In the movie, *Amish Grace,* one of the mothers said her pain was so intense that she forgave the killer but had to do it again the next hour, and the next, and the next.

When we have been hurt deeply, feelings of anger and the desire for revenge may appear over and over again when something reminds us of painful experiences – an encounter with the person who hurt us, anniversaries of tragedies, going to the place where painful events occurred, or just being in a down mood.

When we forgive, we make a commitment to do whatever we need to do to keep overcoming the negative thoughts and feelings and behaviors associated with the hurtful event. Keep trying until you achieve the forgiveness you need. When you do, you can find peace.

A New Beginning – Reconciliation

Forgiveness is the answer to almost all relationship problems. Forgiveness is also the foundation for reconciliation. Some couples have a pattern of giving in and reconciling without forgiving. They reconcile but keep their feelings of resentments and anger. Eventually, these negative feelings may bankrupt their marriages. Then these couples may say, "We just don't love one another any more," or "We just grew apart."

Once we have forgiven, we can decide whether to reconcile with the offending person. A decision about whether to reconcile needs to be based on a rational reason rather than on anger, resentment, fear, or a desire to punish. Or passion.

When we reconcile we restore the emotional closeness we felt before the offense. One strategy for reconciling is to begin with an intention to become close again. Then ask, "What do I need to do to make this the kind of close relationship I want it to be?" Then adjust your thoughts, feelings, and behaviors to support your intention.

Once you have decided to reconcile, eliminate negative thoughts about the offense. Continuing to brood about the past offense will only fuel the negative feelings you need to overcome. Replace negative thoughts with positive thoughts, especially memories of fond times together. Fond memories lead to good feelings and intimacy.

Intimacy is based on positive feelings. Feelings of love make people want to be close. If you want a close relationship, focus on loving thoughts and feelings. Then reach out to your partner.

Intimacy is created with behaviors such as spending time together, taking walks together, working in the garden together, talking about the relationship and events in our lives, smiling at one another, holding hands, saying, "I love you," expressing appreciation, and occasional romantic interludes.

Most of us have some intimacy rituals that have worked for us in the past. Almost any activity that is productive and involves togetherness can be an intimacy builder. These behaviors help us maintain close relationships. They can also help us recover our feelings of closeness after arguments or other problems.

When we do not feel close, we can engage in behaviors that cause us to feel close. If you do not feel like holding hands, do it anyway. Soon you will feel close again.

A Final Challenge

For many of us, forgiving people who have hurt us is one of the hardest challenges we ever face. I am no exception. I know what it is like to be hurt and what it is like to harbor the grudges. I had to struggle with my own forgiveness issues as I wrote this chapter. While my work on this chapter confronted me with challenges it also provided sources of courage and inspiration.

My heart was touched by the depth of the grief of the

Amish parents, and I was inspired by their courage. I was touched by the way they followed their faith even when it was hardest. I know they could have never coped with a loss so great if they had not been able to forgive. In the midst of their deepest grief, these courageous people were able to reach out and support the family of the killer during their time of grief.

I was inspired by the bold forgiveness of Walter Everett, a United Methodist minister, who was able to rely on his faith to lead him through his darkest hours.

Walter Everett's story is even more inspiring when we realize that the killer, Mike Carlucci, was described as a life-long bully and drug addict. To make Everett's pain worse, Carlucci made a deal with the court and received only a five-year sentence.

But because of Everett's forgiveness, Carlucci's life was transformed. When Carlucci read Everett's words, "I forgive you," he prayed for forgiveness. He said no one had ever said, "I forgive you," to him before.

Everett visited Carlucci several times in prison. About three years after he was put in prison, Everett testified at Carlucci's parole hearing asking for his early release, and it was granted. Everett and Carlucci began speaking to churches and community groups about the benefits of forgiveness. In 1994, Everett officiated at Carlucci's wedding.

Today Everett and Carlucci continue to speak at universities, churches, and community groups about the healing power of forgiveness for both the forgiven and the forgiver.

"I can never forget what happened to Scott," Everett said. "It has forever changed my life. But when I look at Mike, I don't see someone who hurt Scott. I see somebody whose life has been changed by God. And I celebrate that."

I have decided that if these people could forgive such deep injustices, I can surely forgive the small offenses I sometimes encounter from friends and relatives, even strangers. By having done my own forgiveness work I have also experienced the freedom that forgiving gives to the forgiver. I hope those whom I have offended will forgive me and experience the freedom.

I do hope that as a result of the inspiration of people like the Amish parents and Walter Everett, we can all learn to be better forgivers. I also hope we can experience the benefits of forgiving and being forgiven. I also hope others can experience the benefits of being forgiven.

Points to Remember

- Forgiveness is pardoning someone whom we believe has offended or harmed us in some way. It is a decision based on a thought. Forgiveness is always the right thing to do and it is always psychologically and emotionally healthy because it is the only way we can heal the pain in our hearts and overcome feelings of anger, resentment, and hate.
- Reconciliation is the process of restoring the emotional closeness that was reduced or destroyed when someone hurt of offended us. When family members reconcile they can be close again.
- No marriage or family can survive without forgiveness. It does not matter how much people may love one another, their love and their relationship will be destroyed if they cannot forgive.
- Forgiveness is one of the most difficult challenges many people ever face. It involves: making a decision to forgive (thought), giving up feelings of anger and resentment, giving up intentions to get even or to get revenge, and not engaging in unkind behaviors.
- To forgive we need to: (1) begin with prayer, meditations, and affirmations, (2) analyze the event or events, (3) look at the positives, (4) get in touch with what we believe, (5) focus on your goals, (6) develop

a healing strategy, (7) overcome fear, (8) overcome cultural influences, (9) make a decision and take action, and (10) follow through.

- Decide whether reconciliation is appropriate. If so, restore the closeness in the relationship by engaging in behaviors that promote closeness.
- We can all be inspired by the experiences of people who have forgiven the seemingly impossible.
- When we forgive we can heal and find peace.

Affirmations

- Forgiveness of myself and others releases me from the pains of the past.
- With God's help, I am a good forgiver.
- Forgiveness is the answer to almost every human problem. I forgive and I set myself free.
- I am a kind, loving and forgiving person.
- I forgive myself and I find peace.
- God is helping me as I forgive people who have hurt me and I am thankful.
- I receive forgiveness from people whom I have hurt and I am thankful.
- I am so thankful that the Spirit of God is leading me as I forgive myself and as I forgive _____.
- I forgive myself and others as God forgives me.

Helpful Exercises

Forgive One Thing Exercise

Identify a situation in which you perceive yourself to have been harmed or offended by a friend or family member. Make a decision to do your best to forgive this one thing. Follow the forgiveness process below.

1. Begin with prayer, meditation, and affirmations.

2. Analyze the event or events. What happened? Be specific and stick to the facts.

3. Describe the positive qualities of the person who offended you. Describe your part in causing this problem to occur?

4. Describe what you believe about forgiveness. What do Jesus words, "Forgive us our debts (trespasses) and we forgive our debtors" (those who trespass against us) mean?

5. Who is the person who offended you and what is your goal for your relationship him or her?

6. Develop a healing strategy that will help you understand the person and event that are causing the problem in a positive or helpful way.

7. What fear is making forgiveness difficult? What might happen if you forgive? If you do not forgive? How can you overcome the fears?

8. What beliefs about life and relationship or what

cultural influences are making forgiveness difficult in this situation? How can you overcome them?

9. Make a decision about forgiveness and take action. What do you need to do to "get the ball rolling"?

10. Follow through. Keep trying to achieve your goal even if you have to try over and over. What can you do to help you keep trying until you succeed? What supports do you have available to help you?

11. Make a decision about whether it is appropriate to reconcile. If reconciliation is feasible, what can you do to break through the distance and reestablish closeness?

If you have difficulty completing the forgiveness process, do as much as you can. Keep trying. Start again and go as far as you can.

When you have completed this process, think of other forgiveness needs and, one by one, begin working on them.

To Think About

What do you believe about the following verses?
- The words from the Lord's Prayer, "Forgive us our debts as we forgive our debtors." (Matthew 6:12).
- When Peter asked Jesus about how many times to forgive his brother, Jesus replied, "Until seventy times seven."(Matthew 18:21-22).

Notes

The story about the church bell came from a sermon preached in a Methodist church in Adaton United Methodist Church, Starkville, Mississippi. It was a story told in a sermon but did not identify the minister who preached it.

The story about Walter Everett and Mike Carlucci from: (www.thejourneyofhope.blogspot.com/2009/02/forgiveness-in-the-face-of-unforgiveable-rev.html; www.willsworld.com; www. Adatonchurch.com/docs/frgiveness.pdf).

Information about Nelson Mandela and the Union of South Africa was based on the movie *Invictus* and numerous articles and quotations from internet resources including Nelson Mandela Quotes, Wikipedia, www.africansuccess.org, www.Africa.com, www.brainyquotes.com.

Information about the Amish people and the tragedy came from the movie *Amish Grace,* several on-line discussions, and from Hildebrand and others, *Knowing and Serving Diverse Families*. 3rd Edition, 2008.

CHAPTER 9

CONCLUSION: THE CHALLENGE

In *The Power of Now,* Eckhart Tolle tells the following story.

> A beggar had been sitting by the side of a road for over thirty years. One day a stranger walked by. "Spare some change?" mumbled the beggar, mechanically holding out his old baseball cap. "I have nothing to give you," said the stranger. Then he asked: "What's that you are sitting on." "Nothing," replied the beggar. "Just an old box. I have been sitting on it for as long as I can remember." "Ever looked inside?" asked the stranger. "No," said the beggar. "What's the point? There's nothing in there." "Have a look inside," insisted the stranger. The beggar managed to pry open the lid. With astonishment, disbelief and elation, he saw that the box was filled with gold.

Like the old beggar in Tolle's story, we all have a box of gold within our reach. All we have to do is open the old box and claim the treasure.

Where families are concerned, many people have learned how to open the box. Husbands and wives who are happily married. Mothers, fathers, and children who have productive relationships. Researchers have found that there are many happy couples and strong families.

When researchers ask members of strong families for the secrets of their success, most of them tell us they are committed to their families and to one another. Many of them also tell us that a strong religious orientation is an important strength of their families. These people have learned that the Tools of the spirit—commitment, faith and hope, love and grace, respect and honor, and forgiveness and reconciliation—are their best resources for marital and family success.

Many people are still searching for the secrets of success. They do not seem to know that their treasure—and successful families are our treasure—is right within the old box they are sitting on. Or, perhaps they do not know how to open the box and claim the treasure. Our society has lost touch with the idea that the core elements of the Christian religion are our most important resources for creating successful families.

But the treasure is ready to be claimed and the Tools or the Spirit are our best resources for opening the box. I am going to end this book with a challenge.

If you would like to prepare for a successful relationship, improve an already strong family, or revitalize a troubled marriage or family, begin with an unwavering commitment. No one can create a happy marriage without a solid commitment. Then, add faith in marriages and families and in your ability to create them. Put your faith into action (hope) by doing your very best to apply these spiritual principles in your relationships every day.

Express your love to your family members by giving and serving rather than by seeking to receive or be served. Accept your family members the way they are (grace). Remember that your family members are children of God, created in the divine image, and they deserve to be respected and honored at all times. Forgive your loved ones when they make mistakes, and reach out to restore the emotional closeness when you are feeling distant or separated (reconciliation).

If you use the Tools of the Spirit, you can succeed. Blessings to you on your journey toward happy marriages and strong families.

REFERENCES CITED

Amish Grace. Lifetime Movie Network, 2010.

Anonymous. Cherokee Proverb, *Tale of Two Wolves.*

Anonymous. www.adatonchurch.org/Docs/Forgiveness.pdf.
Sermon preached at Adaton United Methodist Church in
Adonton, Mississippi.

Brigman, Kelley. Religion and Family Strengths: Implications
for Mental Health Professionals. *Topics in Family
Psychology and Counseling*, 1992: 1(1): 39-52. January.

Brigman, Kelley. Religion and Family Strengths: an Approach
to Wellness. *Wellness Perspectives: Journal of Individual,
Family, and Community Wellness*, 1984:1(2):3-9.

Brigman, Kelley. Churches Helping Families. *Family
Perspective*, 18(2):77-84. Spring 1984.

Brigman, Kelley, and Barbara R. Keating. Religious Attitudes
and Family Strengths: Examining the Relationship.
Unpublished research report, 1996.

Brigman, Kelley. *Marriage: A Simple Guide to Success.*
Mankato, Minnesota: Purple's Edge Media, 2008.

Craddock, Fred B. (ed by Mike Graves and Richard F. Ward).
Craddock Stories.
St. Louis, Missouri: Chalice Press, 2001.

Craddock, Fred B. *The Cherry Log Sermons*. Louisville:
Westminster/John Knox, 2001.

Doherty, William. *Take Back Your Marriage: Sticking
Together in a World That Pulls Us Apart.* New York: The
Guilford Press, 2001.

Doherty, William J. *Intentional Marriage: Your Rituals Will Set You Free*. Banquet Keynote Address, Fourth Annual Smart Marriages Conference, Denver, Colorado, July 1, 2000.

Dreikurs, Rudolf R. *Fundamentals of Adlerian Psychology.* Chicago: Alfred Adler Institute, 1950.

Enright, Robert. *Forgiveness is a Choice: A Step-by-Step Process for Resolving Anger and Restoring Hope.* Washington, DC: American Psychological Assoication, 2001.

Fillmore, Lowell (Compiler). *The Unity Treasure Chest: A Selection of the Best of Unity Writings*. New York: Hawthorn Books, 1957.

Fireproof, Samuel Goldwin Films, 2008.

Fromm, Erich. *The Art of Loving.* New York: Harper and Row, 1956.

Gottman, John, and Nan Silver. *The Seven Principles for Making Marriage Work*. New York: Three Rivers Press, 1999.

Gottman, John and Nan Silver, a. *Why Marriages Succeed or Fail . . . and How You Can Make Yours Last.* New York: Fireside, 1994.

Grayson, Henry. *Mindful Loving: 10 Practices for Creating Deeper Connections.* New York: Gotham Books, 2003.

Hawthorn, Nathaniel. *The Great Stone Face.*

Hildebrand, Verna; Phenice, Lillian; Gray, Mary; and Hines, Rebecca. *Knowing and Serving Diverse Families*. 3rd Edition. Princeton, NC: Merrill, 2008.

Holy Bible. Quotations from the Bible are from a variety of versions.

Institute for American Values. *Why Marriage Matters: Twenty-Six Conclusions From the Social Sciences (2nd Ed).* New York: Institute for American Values, 2005.

Institute for American Values, Center for Marriage and Families. *What Is America's Most Serious Social Problem?* Fact Sheet No. 1, February 2006.

Institute for American Values, Center for Marriage and
    Families. *The Scholarly Consensus on Marriage,* Fact
    Sheet No. 2, February 2006.
Institute for American Values, Center for Marriage and
    Families. *Does Divorce Make People Happy? Findings
    from a Study of Unhappy Marriages.* Report, June 2002,
    Executive Summary.
Invictus, Warner Brothers, 2009.
Jayson, Sharon. Blankenhorn: A family guy with a cause. *USA
    Today,* March 14, 2007.
Kraybill, Donald B., Steven M. Nolt, and David L. Weaver-
    Zercher. *Amish Grace: How Forgiveness Transcended
    Tragedy.* San Francisco: Josey-Bass, 2007.
Love, Patricia and Steven Stosny. *How to Improve Your
    Marriage Without Talking About It.* New York: Broadway
    Books. 2007.
McTaggart, Lynne. *The Intention Experiment: Using Your
    Thoughts to Change Your Life and the World.* New York:
    Free Press, 2006.
Meyer, Roger A. Development of a Committed-Nominal
    Religious Attitude Scale. A paper presented to the
    Southeastern Psychological Association. New Orleans,
    Louisiana, March 1976).
National Council on Family Relations. Fact Sheet, April 2003
    Minneapolis, Minnesota.
Nolt, Steven M. "Why the Amish Forgave a Killer." A speech
    by Steven M. Nolt, Professor of History, on Monday,
    October 1, 2007 at Goshen College
Peck, M. Scott. *The road Less Traveled: A New Psychology of
    Love, Traditional Values and Spiritual Growth.* New York:
    Simon and Schuster, 1978.
Piper, Wally, George Hauman and Doris Hauman. *The Little
    Engine That Could.* New York: Platt and Munk, 1976.
Seligman, Martin E. P. *Authentic Happiness: Using the New*

Positive Psychology to Realize Your Potential for Lasting Fulfillment. New York: Free Press, 2002.

Simmons, Gary. *The I of the Storm: Embracing Conflict, Creating Peace.* Unity Village, Missosuri: Unity House, 2004.

Sittler, Joseph. Marriage and snow on the mountain, from *Grace Notes and Other Fragments.* Philadelphia: Fortress Press, 1981.

Stosny, Steven. *Love Without Hurt: Turn Your Resentful, Angry, or Emotionally Abusive Relationship into a Compassionate Loving One.* Philadelphia: De Capo Press, 2006.

Tolle, Eckhart.. *The Power of Now: A Guide to Spiritual Enlightenment.* Novato, California: New World Library, 1999.

Townley, Edward. *The Secret According to Jesus: Living a Joyful Life.* Dallas, Texas: Brown Books Publishing Group, 2007.

Waite, Linda and Gallagher, Maggie. *The Case for Marriage: Why Married People Are Happier, Healthier, and Better Off Financially.* New York: Doubleday, 2000.

Wallerstein, Judith, and Sandra Blakeslee. *The Good Marriage: How and Why Love Lasts.* New York: Warner Books, 1995.

Williamson, Marianne. *A Return to Love: Reflections on the Principles of a Course in Miracles.* New York: Harper Collins, 1993.

Wilson, James Q. In *What Is America's Most Serious Social Problem?* Institute for American Values, Fact Sheet, No. 1, February 2006.

Wright, N. T. *After You Believe: Why Christian Character Matters.* New York: Harper One, 2010.